Just Call Her

Jane

II

Catriona Murray

JUST CALL HER

JANE

The author acknowledges that her
memories are imperfect but
has shared them to the best of her
knowledge. All names of persons, except for the
author's family, have been changed.

ISBN: 9781983354502

For Finn

VI

Table of Contents

ACKNOWLEDGEMENTS

First and foremost, my dearest friend and mentor, Georgia Brown, without whom this book would never have been completed - the early pages would still be sitting, lost and forgotten. Thank you for your ceaseless encouragement, for all your time reading, re-reading, and correcting. Above all thank you for showing me that I could write.

Thank you to my beloved Dott.ssa Anna Pesci who nurtured me and gave me the tools to find my way.

Shelagh – my mother – I know how much you loved me.

Thank you also to my sister in law, Elena Matteini. You gave me faith that this book was valid and insisted that I should publish.

Most importantly, I would never be where I am today without my husband Lorenzo. You have stood by me, unfailingly, and lived my story with me. Thank you for your immeasurable patience and love. And lastly, my three most cherished children, Camilla, Tom and Anna - thank you for giving meaning and happiness to my life.

x

PROLOGUE

I am in the attic of the nursing home where my adoptive father, has just died. His body is still in the morgue. I have organized his cremation. Here in the attic, I am not alone. My birth mother who I have recently found is with me. We are the only two people in the attic.

I find a tap lying on the floor. A metal tap. "This will do," I think. "It's heavy enough." I hold it above my head ready to take a swing.

What I need to take a swing at is a padlock on a metal filing cabinet. Actually I'd say more of a small box really. I see it there lying amongst his possessions – some framed photographs of me, of our family, three or four paintings, his old radio, a long shoe horn – this is all that is left of him. The filing cabinet has caught my eye. Its outside I know so well. Brown metal. Its inside I have never seen. I know there are secrets in here, secrets surrounding my adoption, which I was never allowed to know about.

I have managed to uncover the facts without the aid of any of the files, but now I am desperate to see them. But I can't find the key. Where's the key for the padlock? There's an urgency to open it. I look for a hammer. There isn't one. Then I see the discarded tap.

I take one swing and hear metal hit metal. The padlock flies open. I open the lid. File upon file lies before my eyes. I can search now, at my leisure. No one can tell me I can't.

The owner of the cabinet is no longer my father. It's me. I find a letter. We read together.

NATIONAL CHILDREN ADOPTION ASSOCIATION

(INCORPORATED)

Registered under The Adoption of Children (Regulation) Act 1939

Patron: H.M. QUEEN ELIZABETH THE QUEEN MOTHER

President and Chairman of Executive Committee :
H.R.H. THE PRINCESS ALICE, Countess of Athlone
G.C.V.O., G.B.E.

Vice Chairman :
Mrs. J. E. MONTAGU

General Secretary :
Mrs. D. C. PLUMMER, M.B.E.
to whom all communications
should be addressed

Founder :
THE LATE MISS CLARA ANDREW

**71, KNIGHTSBRIDGE
LONDON, S.W.1**
—

Tel. BELGRAVIA 4436-7

Ref: 18152A

26th July 1965

Mrs. N.J. Murray,
Fairways,
Worplesdon Hill,
Woking,
Surrey.

Dear Mrs. Murray,

CONFIDENTIAL - FOR YOU AND YOUR HUSBAND ONLY.

We are now glad to be able to tell you about a very well-born little girl who will be ready for adoption on Wednesday, 28th July as we have agreed to accept her for an immediate placement from the hospital with adopting parents. We shall be glad to hear from you therefore immediately on receipt of this letter and if you are interested in her, we shall be pleased to arrange an appointment for you and your husband to see her here at 3.15 p.m. on Wednesday, 28th July when you will be able to take her home with you if you like her.

Little "Jane" as she is called at present, was born on 18th July 1965 and weighed 7lbs at birth - she has a perfect medical certificate and has brown hair and blue eyes. Both her parents are young students from Canada (the girl has come over here to have the baby so that their families would not know about the pregnancy). The mother is 19 years of age and is an art student - she is the daughter of a doctor and she has a graduate brother and another sister who has studied art. The mother is 5ft. 5" tall with auburn hair and grey/green eyes and is keen on drawing and painting of all kinds. The father of the little girl is 21 years of age and is an engineering student at McGill University. He is the son of a lawyer and has brown hair and blue eyes - he is 5ft. 11" tall. There is no question of a marriage between this young couple and the mother wishes to have her baby adopted to give her a normal home background and the same chances in life that both she and the father have enjoyed.

We shall look forward to hearing from you, and we hope we shall have the pleasure of introducing your little daughter to you on Wednesday.

Yours sincerely,

General Secretary.

EMY

3

PART ONE

CHAPTER ONE

As a little girl, it seemed to me the most normal thing in the world that I hadn't been born from my mother and father. I had come to them in a different way. It was just the way it was.

What 'coming from your mummy and daddy' meant, I understood: I knew that people came from inside their mummies' tummies and that their daddies had planted a seed and from that seed came a baby. It didn't bother me that I hadn't come to them in this way. In fact, I was relieved that my parents hadn't had to perform this extremely embarrassing but necessary act. I imagined all the mummies and daddies facing each other in a standing position, with their pants round their ankles, doing this sort of desperate fumbling and poking, each having to hold their genitals as close to each others' as possible. I imagined that on deciding that they wanted to make a baby, they then had to go through this utterly undignified ordeal, and that it must be done as quickly as possible so as to not prolong the embarrassment. The embarrassment - that was the worst part. I felt sorry for all of my friends because they had to live with the image of this, while I was the lucky one being able to boast my parents didn't 'do it', because fortunately, I was adopted.

It was 1973 and just before my eighth birthday, I was told I was adopted. However, I cannot, for the life of me, *remember* the moment. There was simply the 'knowing' – as if it had floated into my consciousness by magic - and it was etched there as firmly as the knowledge of existing.

There are so many details of my life from before this time that are crystal clear – eating fish and chips with our parents upstairs because of the flood downstairs like Noah's Ark (the washing machine door had broken), aged three; peeing in my pants at a ballet lesson and knowing for the first time the feeling of shame, aged four; my first real nightmare, aged five; being spanked with a wooden spoon by my mother Shelagh, aged six. But I have no recall of my mother sitting me down to tell me that she was not my real mother, aged eight. I can't remember where we were, how we were, how she told me. I can't remember her words, her tone. Nothing. And above all I have absolutely no idea how it made me feel. It is the most extraordinary blank space in my mind. I think I would have to undergo hypnosis to bring the memory into my conscious world

"I'm going to marry Finn when I'm grown up!" said Rebecca Holmes. Finn was my older brother who was also adopted. We, Rebecca and I, were in the line up in the classroom waiting to go out to play. I was still seven – just - and this was my day school, Red House.

"No you're not!" I retaliated suddenly feeling extremely possessive. "Anyway, you can't because I'm going to marry him!"

"You can't marry your brother!"

"Oh yes I can! *I'm* adopted."

"What's adopted?"

"It means you can marry your brother. When you're *adopted,* you can marry each other if you want when you grow up, because you're not real brother and sister so you are allowed to be husband and wife. And it also means that you're special. I'm very special because I was *chosen.* You weren't chosen so you can't be special. And it also means you're priceless." This word 'priceless' conjured up an image of a price attached to my forehead – something I'd do with the sticky label of an orange or an apple, for the fun of enjoying the stickiness.

"What's priceless?"

7

"Priceless means when they can't say how much you cost because you are so special."

We lived in a house called 'Lower Mill'. It wasn't the first house I can remember, but it was the house we lived in when I learned I was adopted. It was also the place that would hold us together as a family for the next thirty years – a compass from which we could each take our bearings. It was where my identity took root, the nucleus of my childhood. It was also our first house that didn't belong to the government.

My father, Nat, was in the army, and until I was six, we had always lived in small army quarters, usually three-up and three-down. Here had been the fish and chips episode, the ballet lesson, the nightmare, the spank.

But now it was Lower Mill. We wouldn't live in army camps any more. We wouldn't be posted to other places in England or abroad. We would be fixed in one place. This was because Nat was due to retire. Yes I was only six, but my father was already fifty-two and at fifty-five officers had to retire to make way for younger up-and-coming officers. We could settle in our own home for the first time: Lower Mill.

Lower Mill was 'L'-shaped and huge. It was so exciting to have so many bedrooms after our cramped quarters. Stables, garage, woodshed, tool-shed, mill (as in watermill), hall, drawing room, sitting room, study, dining room, utility room, cloakroom, store room – I could go on forever through the whole house.

As for outside, there was no garden to speak of, but about two acres of what I can only describe as ugly wasteland. A wilderness Shelagh called it. There must have been a garden here once as there were still remnants of a vegetable patch. There were box hedges too - their dignity as formal dividers long lost - collapsed and overgrown. But these were the only traces. The rest was all hawthorn - that hostile prickly bush that spreads itself everywhere if left unchecked - and it took up all the remaining space. Yes, quite a wilderness.

Surrounding all of this though, was a river. A timeless motion of water that would bring life and meaning to this dormant and neglected place.

My parents set about the huge task of transforming it into a wild and almost exotic garden, a garden that would become a magical play place for Finn and me.

Finn and I were able to row around the river in a dinghy, or swim or fish. We could catch minnows with a net. The best part was how our dog (my best friend) would put his whole head into the bucket where we'd keep the minnows, and then catch them in his mouth and proceed to eat them. He was a black Labrador called Bran. It made me squeal and jump around in delighted disgust. So I'd catch some more minnows and watch him do it again. We caught trout too, dangling a line over the bridge at the front. I'd squeal again as the fish flopped on the grass gasping, and I couldn't bear to deal with their slippery bodies to unhook them and put them back in the water, so Finn would tell me to stop jumping around, while he would casually do this part for me.

Bran, being a Labrador (they were bred for helping the fishermen pull in their nets in the Atlantic Ocean), adored swimming in the river. We could spend hours throwing in sticks for him to retrieve. He never stopped, and even in the freezing cold months, he would hurl himself forward – plosh. How we delighted watching him.

We too delighted in swimming in the river – as soon as there was a sunny day in the spring, whatever the temperature, in we went. Water up to rib height, tummy held in tight and elbows raised - as if this would avoid the freezing contact for those first few moments - before the icy thrill of the real plunge. The river is where I learned to swim - in the mill pool.

It was also here in this garden on one of the lawns – so magically transformed from that tangle of hawthorn - where I was forced to play not tennis but cricket, a quintessential part of our summer. How many times we had to get on our bicycles to race down the road faster than the current when we'd wacked a ball into the river.

Rebecca Holmes used to come and stay often. Poor Rebecca - she had to know that her parents had done the poking act, and not just once but four times, because Rebecca had three older brothers. Perhaps they'd even been naked. My parents had never seen each other naked. What a shocking thought. Finn and I being naked, wasn't in the least shocking – we had baths together – but the idea of my mother and father being naked together or merely undressing in the same room was beyond me. My parents would (or could) never do such a thing. They didn't share a double bed – one was my father's bed and the other my mother's. The two very austere beds with huge wooden frames stuck out parallel from the wall, distinctly separated, and took up most the space in the room.

This was just the way it was in our home, even if Rebecca Holmes' parents shared a double bed and even if all my friends' parents did too. There wasn't a double bed in our spare room either, just two distinctly separate singles.

It was so strange then, when one day, I found Shelagh preparing the spare bedroom not in the usual way at all. Melanie and Thomas Howard were coming to stay, and there was my mother pushing the two single beds together. She heaved the heavy antique bedside table – so purposeful in its position between the beds – and placed it to one side. "Why are you putting their beds together Mummy?"

"Well they've just got married, so I expect they'd like the beds to be together," came my mother's explanation. She said it as if it were a treat, something special – something they were *allowed* to do - and in that instant I became suspiciously aware that other couples were very happy with bodily contact – it wasn't embarrassing at all, but rather something quite nice.

"Why doesn't Daddy use your bathroom Mummy? Why does he always have to use ours?" I pressed. His habit of padding across the landing to the other bathroom – our bathroom - instead of more appropriately using the one inside their own bedroom, troubled me.

10

"Well, he feels too cramped in my one; he says it's too small. He prefers more space you see." Shelagh justified.

It wasn't that I minded him using our bathroom, but rather, it was the mystery that unsettled me. Now I definitely sensed something was wrong: something was *different* about my parents – a difference which went far beyond my not having come to them in the usual way like everybody else.

CHAPTER TWO

My parents should never have married.

But on 6th February 1952 in the Anglican church of Holy Trinity Brompton, London, these two people tied their fateful knot. They barely knew each other.

On that day, my mother Shelagh was a virgin. Of course for that time, this was nothing unusual, or at any rate, even if you'd already done it before your wedding day, you would have only done it with The One, The One being the man you would choose to marry, and no one else. Anything less, you were cheap, you were a slut, you were loose. Of course there were all sorts of women who violated these myths but Shelagh was 'proper' – and she paid a high price for that.

At just twenty-one, a London debutant ripe for the picking, innocent, beautiful – an Ingrid Bergman beautiful – on this day, my mother walked up the aisle on her father's arm.

Their honeymoon would be three-weeks on board a ship to Hong Kong. Nat, a decorated war veteran and now career officer, had just accepted a posting in Hong Kong. When he asked Shealgh to marry him a few weeks before, it was truly now or never, for he would be gone to the Far East for at least the next four years. She accepted.

On that first night, in the honeymoon suite, alone at last, they'd got into bed together where she expected him to finally make love to her. But nothing happened. He didn't touch her. Rather he turned away, offering his back, and went to sleep. She lay awake thinking that she had done something wrong.

Perhaps they were both on edge; perhaps he was simply too tired. It would all work out the next night.

But the next night the same thing happened. And the next and the next. After dinner each evening, instead of staying with her, or eagerly rushing her back to the cabin, he would leave her alone while he went to play bridge. Shelagh didn't know how to play bridge. She would sit and either wait for him or retire alone to the cabin. Finally one night when she had already gone to bed, shortly after, he came in drunk. He switched the light off, got into bed, and 'performed'. She recounted how losing her virginity was the ugliest experience of her life. He had behaved as if it were a duty he knew had to be done, a job to get over and done with. No soft words, no tenderness. He barely touched her again, even in simple affection, in the forty-five years they were married.

Within just these first few days of her marriage then, on board a ship somewhere in the middle of the Indian Ocean, and leaving everything familiar behind for a new life in a distant and foreign land, she realized she had made the biggest mistake of her life. Worse, there was simply nothing she could do about it. She had made her vows to him.

After six yeas of enduring his coldness, his turning his back on her, both metaphorically and literally, one day, she plucked up courage and left.

By this time they were living in Germany and she had fallen in love with another officer. For two years they had been having an affair. His name was Tom. I gloated (and still do) over one photograph of her, lying up in bed, ruffled and relaxed and happy looking; she is smiling with her arms casually crossed in front of her. In all the other pictures I have of her, I can't help but notice the sadness in her eyes, a kind of sadness that tugged at her from one year to the next. Here, her green eyes look straight at the camera and have an expression in them that I have never seen.

She moved back to London on her own, believing she and her beloved Tom would have a future together. Shelagh couldn't talk to friends about what had happened – perhaps she found her plight too humiliating - so she remained silent and patient. Patient because Tom, still in Germany, could only visit infrequently and briefly – when 'on leave'. But it was worth the wait for she knew she would divorce Nat as soon as it was possible, and would be free to marry Tom, putting her mistake and Nat, behind her.

One day, Tom arrived with devastating news. "Darling!" Like in an old fashioned black and white film like Casablanca I imagined, eyes locked in anguish together, "Darling, we can't marry!"

His father had pleaded with him on his deathbed, that he not marry Shelagh, who would by then, be a divorcee. Tom felt obliged to keep his promise, not to Shelagh, but to his father.

Her world fell apart right there and then – she wanted to die.

So Tom walked out of her life and married someone else, a woman he didn't love, he said, but who was more appropriate in his father's eyes. She was Canadian. Tom left Europe, left the army, left Shelagh and moved to Canada. A new life in the new world.

Bereft, probably traumatised, Shelagh was more alone now, even than in her sterile marriage. She didn't want anyone other than Tom - Tom had been 'The One'. She had no money, no parents to lean on (her mother had early senile dementia, her father was nowhere to be seen, her brother dead), and in the narrow world she lived in, divorce was not merely stigmatized, but punished. She knew that if she divorced Nat, he'd lose his career. Officers then were not allowed to divorce. She couldn't face her own disgrace as a divorcee, one without property or means. She went back to Nat.

On one condition: That they adopt.

In 1964 they adopted a boy whom they named Finn.

In 1965 I became their daughter.

CHAPTER THREE

1975. Dutch Elms line the narrow lane that leads to our house. All over England, Dutch Elms are dying. A tree might fall at any moment across the lane and kill someone driving past or at very least, block the road. They must all be cut down.

I was so relieved that now we would be free of the trees. Ours were set very close together, thick ivy taking over their trunks forming almost a wall; in fact as I remember them, they didn't really resemble trees at all - perhaps there was some form of spindly growths trying hard to be branches at the top, in a suffocated and stunted way, but to me they looked grotesque. They darkened the lane enormously casting grim and terrifying shadows and in the wind they would sway, just slightly, in a ghostly way, and when they swayed they creaked. It was the spookiest thing ever. I tried to avoid walking along this lane at dusk or worse still, in full darkness. The more I told myself to not look, the more my eyes were drawn towards the trees. The thick ivy rustling in the wind became the evil figure moving from behind one tree to another, watching me, following me. Perhaps he was going to pounce on me.

Somebody had to take the dog out before bed. This time I was accompanying my father on his nightly ritual. Everything about my father was a ritual. On went his duffle coat, wellington boots, hat and scarf. Never an item omitted. As we walked along, I held my father's hand. It felt warm and safe, to be linked to him. His hands were always warm. I told him that I was frightened of the dark.

"But there's no need to be frightened of the dark," he said gently. "The dark is your friend."

It seemed a strange thing to think of the dark personified and still more a friend, but I held on in comfortable silence as I pondered the thought. If I didn't like the peculiar separation he kept from my mother, in that moment, I liked him being my father.

There were other Nat rituals that I liked, like having eggs for breakfast on Saturdays and Sundays - poached or scrambled or fried - only cooked by him, the best. "Who's for scram this morning then?" and he'd make them creamy and soft and no one could do it as well as he. Or polishing shoes on Sunday mornings before church. Nat would always have substantial well-made shoes, leather uppers and soles, which would be re-soled or re-heeled by the cobbler so that their life span could be decades. He taught me how to look after the leather. The first thing you must do when you had a brand new pair of shoes, before wearing them, would be to polish them. You must protect new shoes straight away. Sunday mornings before church was shoe polishing time. There was a brush for putting on the polish, then you were to wait a little before taking the other brush for buffing them up – I loved that part watching the opaque part transform into shininess - and then a final extra shine with a soft cloth. A creature of routine, my father never wavered from this weekly habit, and resting our shoes on same spot on top of the washing machine in the utility room, I took comfort in sharing this particular custom.

As with everything else, my father had a routine about going to church too: we went every Sunday. We sat in our same pew. He sang out of tune. He read the lesson occasionally. He shook hands with the vicar. We came home.

For me though, the services were so deadly boring – a weekly discipline one simply had to endure. There was nothing pleasurable about them, and why did everybody have to act so holy just because they were in a church? The only part I liked was the hymns. I liked the melodies and had my favourites. During the hymns, there was also the distraction of my father singing so out of tune, and Finn and I would catch each other's eye. His singing really was terrible – he was tone deaf. (I have since learned that only one per cent of human beings are tone deaf. Many people think they can't sing, but in reality, if you play them a note, the vast majority of people can sing it back to you. Nat was one of those one in a hundred who was unable to do that.) But his singing out of key would break the monotony of the seemingly endless service, and Finn and I could twinkle at each other – our own private language.

If I found my father an amusement, my mother's behaviour in church made me want to shrink from her. I didn't like sitting next to her. I cringed at her devout way, the way she said the Creed, "I believe in one God, the Father Almighty, Maker of heaven and earth...." Or, The Lord's Prayer - "Our Father, who art in heaven...".

I didn't not believe the words; I just wanted her to be more matter of fact in the way she said them. She almost whispered them like she was having an intimate time with them, or like the words were going to rescue her in some way. I knew them by heart of course and out they'd come from my mouth flatly, like reciting a poem I'd had to learn at school, defying her devotion.

"Go and look in there," my mother said one day when she'd just brought me back form school, pointing to the door of the drawing room. "There's a nice surprise."

Surprises were as good as treats. They were even as good as getting a present. My heart leapt. What could it be? In I charged and heard the sound of the television. One couldn't see the television from the door because the fireplace in the centre of the room, divided the room in half. The "smart" end of the drawing room was the bigger and first half, and the television comfy end was on the other side of the fireplace.

"What? What's the surprise?" I said asking my mother who'd followed me in.

"Go round the other side and see," she replied with eyes lighting up in anticipation.

"A colour television!" I shrieked. "A *colour* one! Wow!" I couldn't believe my eyes. It was utterly magical. I'd never seen one before. This new television was small – about thirty-five centimetres square – and box-like. Hence, "What's on the box tonight?"

Nat was sitting in his big armchair – the best position was his – and looked up at me with glee. Then he moved over to the television and bent down. "This is how you change the channels. You see there's this dial here," and as he turned it, the picture that he was viewing disappeared and all one could see was a flashing fuzz of greyness with a loud fizzing noise. Then all of a sudden another channel appeared. It wasn't too difficult as there were only three channels: BBC 1, BBC 2, and ITV.

ITV was the only independent channel and had adverts. How Finn and I loved watching them – better than the programmes sometimes. We would play a game of Guess Which Advert This Is. All I had to do for Nescafé was cup my hands together pretending to be holding precious coffee beans, bring them to my nose for the aroma, put on an earnest expression and Finn would guess it, before I had time to start acting David Niven. Or there was the one for Hamlet cigars. A man is in a photo booth getting his pose ready. He is almost bald with just one lock of long hair left. He is trying to position the lanky but precious single lock from one side of his head to the other, smoothing it down carefully to keep it stuck in position. Finn and I loved acting the daft expressions he made for the pose. The lock falls out of place, the flash goes off, he sticks it back down but his hands are in the way this time. In the end, all four photos are a complete disaster. You feel so sorry for the balding man. But his Hamlet cigars save the day and you are relieved to see bliss wash over his face – all life's disasters fade into insignificance - as he takes his first puff of his Hamlet cigar to the sound of Bach's Air on a G-String.

We were allowed to watch the television only at 4pm for the children's programmes. How I loved them: Hector's House, The Magic Roundabout, Blue Peter, Crackerjack were just some of my favourites. Then there was John Craven's Newsround which was news for children which I only quite liked, and when it was all over, it was the real News, read by either Richard Baker, Robert Dougall or Kenneth Kendall – how familiar these newsreaders were to me – for my father to watch the moment he got home from work.

The wretched news. My mother's mother Dorothy used to come and stay and she too would want to watch the news. She too was deaf like my father. She was ancient and she suffered at least partial dementia. I used to fix my gaze on her and think, "Stop making that serious face because I know you can't understand a word of what you're watching!"

I didn't like Dorothy. 'Gran' we had to call her, not Granny – she didn't want to be called Granny. She'd come for Christmas or Easter or for lunch on her birthday, 17th May. Actually I was a little frightened. She insisted on bidding me goodnight while I was having my evening bath. I couldn't understand why she couldn't be normal and say goodnight after or before my bath, and I dreaded hearing her approach to the bathroom, and always wanted to hide my naked child body from her, so peculiar was her presence.

My father treated her kindly and like the true lady she actually was, but Shelagh found her hard to tolerate. Being deaf she had one of those hearing aids you kept in your pocket that was connected to the gadget in the ear by a wire. She never understood how it worked because she'd never be able to remember Shelagh's explanations, so when she took it out, she had a habit of just pulling the string out of the battery part without switching it off first. The battery would therefore would run out really quickly.

"Mummy you have to *switch   it   off!* Otherwise the battery will run out". Shelagh would shout at poor Gran in a cross and exasperated way.

"Don't tell me what to do! I know how it works perfectly well!"

As a result, half the time the hearing aid wasn't actually working, so that was why I knew she couldn't hear or understand a word of The News.

"If I ever go demented like that, you must shoot me," my mother used to say. She was absolutely serious.

19

This deafness though was the main source of our entertainment. We could fart freely in front of her (as long as it wasn't a SBD - Silent But Deadly) and of course the louder the better - her unchanged expression with the noise of these eruptions right by her ear, was what would send us running out of the room into peals of laughter.

She was a source of entertainment in other ways too. We would imitate her taking her hot chocolate at teatime. The rest of us would have a cup of tea, five o'clock sharp. In the larder we had a tub of Cadbury's dried hot chocolate mix, just for Gran, which stayed there untouched, like an ornament, years after she died. The tub was so big its package boasted enough mix to make one thousand cups of hot chocolate.

I would ask, knowing perfectly well she never drank tea, "Would you like a cup of tea Gran?"

"No dear. I'd prefer hot chocolate." She always wanted a cup and saucer and teaspoon so that she could stir the hot chocolate, as it was always too hot. So Finn and I would purposefully present it to her in a mug.

"Could I have it in a cup and saucer?" And then on we'd push it as far as we could go by 'forgetting' the spoon. We couldn't get over how long she'd stir. We reckoned that because she didn't have a memory she'd forgotten how long she'd been stirring. Round and round went that spoon, tinkle tinkle against the side of the cup.

"Guess who this is?" Stir stir. Tinkle tinkle. Ha ha.

CHAPTER FOUR

When Finn was seven years old, they sent him away. They sent him to boarding school. This was in order to *give him the best chances possible in life.*

In September 1971 we drove him to the new school. Northaw. We were parked in front. Next to the car parked beside us, were two parents trying to console their son - another little new boy. He was crying. His name was Michael. Michael McCloud. He was crying so hard that his whole face was as red as a tomato. I knew exactly why he was crying too. For me - a little girl of six years old - it was awful, jut awful to watch, because the idea of being left like this was nothing short of *terrifying.* Worse still it was about to happen to my own brother.

Unlike Michael McCloud though, Finn didn't cry. We left him and drove off. I looked back through the rear window of the car – our old Hillman – but I couldn't see him. I wondered what he was doing. Was he walking in through the door? Was he being shown in? Was he walking up the stairs? Was he sitting on his bed with all those other beds in the same room? Was he still holding back the tears? But it would be a while before I saw him again – about a month or so before he could have a day home.

It turned out that Finn was happy in the new school, even if he was so young. It was here that his passion for music began. The organist-come-music teacher was called Mr Motram. He was tall – quite giant-like in my eyes – with a lot of hair and a great bushy beard like Hercules. He was ever so enthusiastic about Finn's ear – his ear for music. It was Mr Motram who discovered that Finn had perfect pitch and encouraged him with his singing and his playing. He even allowed Finn to play the school organ - I felt so proud to be the sister of the only boy at school allowed to do this.

The headmaster of Northaw (my best friend Rebecca's father) had previously been headmaster of Colet Court preparatory school in London. In 1967 Colet Court had commissioned an unknown young composer by the name of Andrew Lloyd-Webber, along with lyricist Tim Rice, to write a piece for the school. The piece resulted in the musical '*Joseph and The Amazing Technicolour Dreamcoat*'. After its appearance in the school it was then considered good enough to be put on real stage. The real stage was in our town, Salisbury. It was so successful here that it later reached the West End. As a family we went to see it in Salisbury. My first musical. I was mesmerized. Finn and I loved it so much so that we bought the score and the LP from a small music shop in town.

So it was in the school holidays, that we'd spend hours singing our way through '*Joseph*'. Joined by a musical, we hid ourselves away in a room – the music room – at the end of the house. Here was our grand piano, all over its mahogany top, books and photographs. I loved the wedding photograph of my demented grandmother, Dorothy. She didn't look at all demented here – beautiful in fact - with her huge dreamy eyes and bobbed hair. There she was in black and white wearing a delicate headpiece - an ornate cap, trimmed with dripping beads of glass – which adorned her flawless complexion. She caught my eye every time I entered the room. How could she ever have transformed from this to what she was now, or more impossibly still, how could Gran have ever been like *this*?

On the windowsill, was our old gramophone. It was grey and box-like just like the television, and one could close the lid and pick it up like a suitcase. It worked perfectly and we would put on our LP, place the needle on the exact groove in the vinyl we wanted, and listen or sing along.

Finn played the piano and cello. I too played the piano and we'd sometimes give mini concerts to our parents. The best part of this was making the programme. Shelagh had an

Olivetti typewriter - mechanical of course – and I learned to tap the keys to produce inked letters on the page. A bell would sound when you reached the end of the line, so as to remind you to pull the carriage return lever. We'd proudly hand the programme - there was one for each parent as I used the carbon paper to make a copy - and then the 'concert' would begin. Finn would play a piece, then I would play mine, then we'd manage a duet - sometimes he on the cello and I the piano, or both on the piano - and then we'd do the singing together. Without me, there would never have been a programme, but without Finn, there would never have been a concert.

There was a Christmas carol too we'd sing over and over, 'Oh Little Town of Bethlehem'. I would sing the melody and Finn the harmony. Most Christmas's when we were still quite small, less than ten years old I suppose, we would visit Florence, first cousin to Nat. She was tiny, with her grey hair tied up in a bun. She lived in a cottage that looked like it came out of a fairy tale book with a wobbly roof and latticed windows and smelling of ancient things. I can remember watching her as Finn and I would sing to her this carol - no accompaniment, just our child voices - and I couldn't take my eyes off her because while she listened, she would close her eyes and look like she was in heaven.

If Finn was the musician, I don't really know what I was. Finn's little sister I suppose. I was perfectly happy tagging along with the singing and if I was any different from him, I certainly didn't give it a thought. We didn't look like each other one little bit, but then for me, *not* looking alike was normal – it was to be expected. To look alike - something I knew everybody else had – was unknown territory. Yes I knew we weren't blood brother and sister, but these were just words, not feelings. He was certainly brother enough to me.

Looking so different had no further consequences. Finn's eyes were brown – great pools of sensitivity that could fill up like water emerging from deep inside a well - and mine were green. I had quite a pointed chin and prominent cheekbones, whereas Finn had a beautifully shaped jaw. He would go brown as a button in the sun - my mother used to say - whereas I had fair skin and freckles. I was skinny and Finn started getting quite plump. Finn was a blond child and I was mousy-brown. And then there were Finn's hands: he was born with beautiful narrow elegant hands with fingers that went on forever. Some people have legs that go on forever but with Finn, it was his fingers. He could span them so wide, well wider than an octave on a piano. They were made for music. This was always commented on by my mother. My hands weren't like that at all. I didn't have horrible hands - just normal, quite neat little hands and my fourth fingers slightly bent inwards. Shelagh used to comment on that too with a vague wondering of where the bend might have come from. I didn't think about it - they were just there as a part of me, and, unlike my mother, I didn't think to attribute to anything at all. They were only a couple of fingers after all.

I felt perfectly comfortable not looking like Finn and if anybody made the strange observation that we looked like each other (a conclusion people jump to if they don't know you're adopted), I felt almost obliged to correct their misguided observation.

In contrast, if I received the same comment regarding me and my mother, I was pleased – I almost glowed inside. I didn't want to correct them, not because I was ashamed of being adopted - that part I held up proudly – but because I *wanted* to look like her. She had a very slight bump in her nose and I had that too. We both had brown hair, and both had green eyes. (Never mind she had quite giant hands and no little bent fingers.) If I couldn't escape the fact that I hadn't grown inside of her, I could still make myself feel as if I had. A bit like believing in fairy-tales.

CHAPTER FIVE

September 1973. I was standing with my back against a very large arched wooden door of my new boarding school called Hanford. Large enough for a lorry to pass through. My parents had brought me and left. I would not see them again for another month. The separation would be felt more if one's parents came back 'too quickly' - we would settle more easily without the hindrance of seeing our parents. So a visit for the first three weeks of term was not allowed. I was eight years old. I didn't cry.

I stood there like a wallflower not knowing what to do. There was a girl standing next to me staring at me. I stared back. "What's your name?" But these were words only in my head. I just couldn't quite get them out, and even though I could feel her wishing them from me, they stayed glued to the inside of my mouth. So we just carried on staring at each other in silence.

Then it was time for my first night at my new school. All one hundred and twenty little girls were allocated dormitories, and a list was put up on the big arched door at the beginning of each term. It became a tense moment looking at that list to see where you'd been put, and more importantly, who with. Most dormitories were named after English male poets with four, six, seven, eight or so beds in each. My first new dormitory was called 'South', not a poet, but just because of its place in the building. 'South' had seven beds in it and mine was at the far end pressed up against the wall. I can remember not being able to get to sleep and this was a strange and new thing in itself. When the matron came in to check on all of us, the girl nearest the door told the matron that she couldn't get to sleep. Then the girl in the bed next to her said the same. 'Is there anyone else awake?' It wasn't said harshly; on the contrary her tone was understanding, soft and inviting. I so wanted to speak out but I felt too far away, too small, too insignificant, too frightened, and just huddled further down under my bedclothes pretending to be asleep. I listened to every word of the dialogue with the matron.

"Imagine sheep jumping over a fence. As you watch them, count them," she said. "That helps you fall asleep." I gave it a try but I couldn't even focus on the image let alone count the wretched animals. It seemed a completely useless way of trying to fall asleep.

Two nights later I was moved to another dormitory called Shakespeare. I don't remember asking to be moved but I believe I was more comfortable.

It was here in this dormitory a few months later, that we were punished for squirting toothpaste onto the ceiling. There was a girl called Lizzie, Elizabeth Burrage, who had an idea: we should each stand on our beds, hold the tube of toothpaste above our heads, jump and squeeze at the same time. Up went the blobs and landing on the ceiling. We carried on and in our excitement, before we knew it, the whole ceiling was covered in a decorative array of squirts. We thought they wouldn't notice.

The punishment was to clean out teeth with salt for a week.

I used to suffer terribly every evening when it came to having your hair 'passed'. Worse than the salt. That meant you had to brush your hair so well that a fine comb would be able to be run through every part of your whole head. This would be put to the test by the matron and my hair being so fine, always had knots, even after I'd brushed and triple brushed it and she would pull, oh so hard, it always hurt.

We had to read our Bibles in bed for the first fifteen minutes of reading time, and then were allowed to change over to, 'own books.' In the summer, it was still broad daylight when it was 'lights out' so all the shutters were tightly closed casting the room into complete darkness. Once, the shutter had been left a crack open by mistake, and fortuitously, right by my bed. It gave just enough light for me to carry on reading the book I was so engrossed in: 'A Little Princess' by Frances Hodgson Burnett. I was enthralled with the little Sara who'd been more or less abandoned by her parents and left in a boarding school and then had to become a servant because her father had died and there was nobody to pay the fees.

Every single piece of clothing, every pair of underpants, every sock, every shirt, had to have your name sewed into it. At the beginning of term, when we opened our trunks to unpack, nothing was   allowed to be put away until it had all been checked. That meant holding the list in your hand and laying out on the bed item by item. Ten pairs pants. Ten pairs socks. Three warm skirts. Five long sleeved shirts, and down to: One hairbrush. One comb. One toothbrush. One tube toothpaste. One laundry bag. My nametapes were written: C.C. Murray. That is how my nickname was born: 'CC'. I was thereafter always called CC and never Catriona. Fortunately in the next school I went to, my mother ordered my nametapes as: Catriona Murray so 'CC' was dropped. At home Finn always called me Cat and that has in fact been the nickname that has always stuck and CC became a secret name reserved only for my time at Hanford School.

Baths were twice a week and shared with one other girl. One of the bathrooms on the upper floor had two baths in it so there were four of us in there having our bath one evening. We had to wait for the water of the bath before to run out and as I stood there, I remember saying to my friends that I needed to do a pee.

"Do it in the bath! Do it in the bath! Go on!" The matron had gone out in that moment and all three were daring me to do this defiant act of peeing into the bath.

"I can't!" I cried. But they egged me on so much that I got into the bath, the one on the left, now empty, crouched down, opened my legs and performed. The three of them squealed with delight as they watched in amazement while my pee gushed out all over the bottom of the empty bath. I got back out, rinsed it all away, put the plug in and we started running our next bath.

Then the matron came back and the three of them started giggling.

"What is it? What are you laughing at?" She questioned lightly. But instead of just saying, 'nothing, nothing', they went on and on giggling. The matron became curious at this point.

I will never forget the moment of betrayal when a girl called Halcyon, all primly sitting in the other bath on the left sang in a taunting way,

"Mi-iss, Mi-iss,
Did a pi-iss,
In the ba-a-a-th," and was looking straight at me as she sang her dirty little rhyme.

"Is this true Catriona?" said the matron.

I couldn't lie to save my life. No one defended me and I was immediately sent to the head matron, Miss Lucker.

"Well, Catriona, do you do this sort of thing at home?" I shook my head. The force of shame held my head down and I cast my eyes to the hairbrush that I was clutching on to, as if I might discover the solution to my plight there. I was told to go straight to my dormitory, sent off like a dog being given an order. I obeyed.

By and large my boarding school was a respectful and gentle place though. I don't remember any real suffering. Rules were rules – there were rules at home too – so there was no space to believe one was being hardly done by. The only real suffering was being taken *back* to school each term – how I hated those moments. My stomach would lurch so much that I wanted to be sick, my heart would beat faster and faster as we approached the driveway, my eyes waiting for the big ancient building to come into view and then, once round the corner, no turning back, almost a relief to see that seemingly vast Jacobean mansion, my other life, my other family of sorts, waiting to bring me in and enfold me into its separate and quite peaceful arms.

As we wouldn't see our parents very often – about once every four weeks, on Sundays, we would all have to sit around long trestle tables in the big main hall to write our letters home to them.

"*Dear Mummy and Daddy, I am having a nice time. Yesterday I played netball and I actually scored a goal and........*"

A teacher would come around checking them through – spelling, punctuation - and we'd hand them in to be posted. We'd receive letters too from home, and although my mother's letters meant very little to me – just words on a page - my mother was good about writing every week.

"*Darling Missy-Moo,*

Thank you for your nice and interesting letter last week. That's wonderful you scored a goal in netball.

I hope you are happier now in the dorm and don't mind any more they put you again in Shakespeare. I expect next term you'll be in another dorm.

Unfortunately, Bran has not been very well and we had to take him to the vet. He will have a small operation, but there's nothing to worry about. He will be pleased to see you again when you next come home. It's not long now. We will be there to collect you next Saturday at 12 noon and you can spend the night at home. Won't that be nice? The daffodils are coming out now and the garden is looking pretty. Finn won't be home this time but you will have the same half term later.

Lots of love from Mummyxxxxxxx

CHAPTER SIX

They say that separation is a trauma for a child. Yes I knew the feeling of anxiety - a panicky feeling about being left - but it wasn't just for myself that I felt it. I felt it more for Finn.

He was thirteen now and we were taking him to his new boarding school, now much further away in London. Harrow School. After a two-hour drive we arrived at a forbidding-looking Victorian building - his house - red bricks, blackened by London traffic, right there on the side of the road. He would share a room with two other boys. We all three came into his room with him. It seemed cold, unfriendly and Spartan. What a far cry from our home. I couldn't believe he was going to be left here; how could he bear it? I was hurting inside for him. How cruel and wrong it seemed. I felt helplessness and grief. Grief for him being left in this place, and grief for witnessing him losing a part of us.

He couldn't even speak as we said goodbye. I couldn't understand why it had to be like that, but said nothing as we drove back home. I just wanted him back in the car next to me so that the pain would go away.

I learned much later, in my adult years, that he was unhappy at this school. I sensed it at the time too. He became a little overweight - uncomfortable in his skin - and I knew they bullied him. A torture going back each term. He never said a word. He just bore it, silently. There was no choice. You didn't talk about things like that. Besides, we were just kids – no one asked us to express our feelings.

We didn't talk about being adopted either – we were joined by a silent knowing – knowledge of some far greater separation.

What I also learned much later, was that Finn could remember every detail of being told he was adopted. He was nine years old. Shelagh sat him down on the edge of his bed, and explained to him how she wasn't his real mother. I wasn't his real sister. Had this been the conversation she had had with me too? As he had listened, he must have born the unbearable. Had I born this too? But Finn could remember what he felt, and that sense of both abandonment and betrayal would cast its indelible shadow over him forever.

I held up the fact of being adopted like a prize – I was *chosen,* I was special - and brandished the fact of it, like being top of the class. Unlike me, Finn, felt a very real sense of abandonment by his real mother - unworthy of her: he must be flawed if she didn't want to keep him, and she certainly couldn't have loved him if she did *that*. From one moment to the next, Shelagh was no longer who she had always been – she was not his real mother. His real mother was another whom he would never meet, never see, never know.

Even if you were eighteen, it was against the law in those days to find your birth mother. (In 1978 the law changed.) The birth mothers could get on with their lives putting their mistake behind them. It was for the best. Finn's mother had been eighteen and 'unable to keep him' – that's what he was told.

It was around the same time that I too was told. I only know this because it matches with the time I started talking about being 'chosen' and 'special'. 'Unable to keep you' were words that stuck, but the event itself has been wiped from my memory. For me it was a fairy tale – my fairy tale - I *had* come from Shelagh (well, in a round-about "chosen" sort of way), and I was special because of it. This was my survival. Finn's deeper understanding crushed him and he would never tell a soul.

I believe that all adoptees are like uprooted trees, taken away and planted in another soil. Some end up planted in soil that comes very close to its original kind, and some not quite so much. But there are others that can only survive in their own soil. They cannot be moved and will never truly grow or thrive if they are. I think this was Finn.

Being adopted is about adapting. The separation and the move, nothing other than a trauma. Some adoptees manage to overcome this to a lesser or greater degree, and put out new roots, allowing themselves to be nurtured by this new soil, so that it becomes their true and rightful place. It is indeed the only place. They become the person they are. They grow and thrive even. That's me.

But Finn was different from me. He never thrived.

They sent him away to Harrow and expected great things from him – he should do well academically after all the things they said at Northaw – how bright he was, how much potential he had. He learned to read at the age of three - genius like - and then he was a whiz at maths, that too from a very early age. Later he could do complicated calculations in his head at great speed. He'd click his fingers in the air with closed eyes, 'Don't tell me, don't tell me....' and then come up with the correct number and a triumphant grin.

But what happened? Here at this prestigious boys' school in London, his self-esteem was sucked out of him. A sense of self-worth depleted from the day Shelagh sat him down on the bed. While he managed to throw himself into music and singing, he gave up studying, and finished school: 'a disappointment'.

If Finn was the failed son in my father's eyes, what was Nat in Finn's? Nat, the father, who was meant to give Finn *better chances in life*. Better chances than if he had remained with his real parents. We were the *chosen* children being given "better" parents who would be able to give us a 'normal' home and a 'normal' background.

Nat. That stiff upper lip, and aversion towards any show of affection, Nat was the man who had a drill, not just taking the dog out or polishing shoes on Sundays, but for *everything*. He boxed his whole life up with useless rules and routines. For instance, he kept a little book in the car and made five columns to each page. He would then write down every time he filled up with petrol: the date, the price per gallon, the number of gallons bought, the total amount spent, and the mileage given on the counter of the speedometer. There seemed no foreseeable purpose to this, for he never made any further calculations, and we'd have to sit there in the petrol station before driving off, while he wrote down his little numbers, chewing his tongue to the side of his cheek as he wrote. He'd spend ages in the bathroom too – that place he'd patter off to in the middle of the night - never of course forgetting to put on his bedrooms slippers and dressing gown. During the day, he'd take his wireless in with him – a wireless, never a radio – and because he was so deaf, it would be on full blast so that we could all hear the news followed by The Archers that filtered through the floorboards to the kitchen below. Finn and I could never understand what could keep a person in a bathroom for so long.

"You know Daddy doesn't have any parents Cat?" Cat was the nickname Finn had adopted for me. The idea of my father having parents was impossible to imagine – he was so old himself.

" I know. We've only got Gran." I replied. "Mummy said his mother died when he was only a baby so we should feel sorry for him never having a mother."

"Yes and *his* Daddy died when he was twelve, so he was an orphan."

"What's an orphan?"

"It's when you don't have any parents, so someone else has to look after you. So Daddy got looked after by his aunt. You know Florence?"

"Yes."

"Well it was *her* mother, the aunt who looked after him. And you know what she was called?"

"Nope. No idea."

"The Ant!" I could tell Finn wanted to tell me why she was called The Ant.

"She was even shorter than Florence, so she was so short that they called her The Ant as she was only knee high to a bee!"

33

Knee high to a bee. I liked that expression.

When I was twelve, it was also my turn for the change of school. No longer dormitories with nine little beds, no longer little girls sharing baths or squirting toothpaste onto ceilings. It was big girls' school - a school where girls had breasts, like mothers. I felt tiny. A repeat feeling of my first night at Hanford. Now, Sherborne School For Girls.

My housemistress was called June. June Taylor. Tall, elegant, attractive, a little scary. She was famous for her bad breath. Some evenings we were allowed to watch television. Top of the Pops on Thursday evenings was a favourite of everybody's. We drooled over Adam Ant and The Police, had a laugh over Shakin' Stevens, and bought the albums of Blondie, Fleetwood Mac, The Pretenders, Meat Loaf, Supertramp, Simon and Garfunkel. You could even buy singles if you only wanted just the one song – Dexy's Midnight Runners' "Come on Eileen" or "Don't You Want Me" by The Human League - and we had a record player in the sitting room where we were allowed to play them.

There was a BBC comedy show starring a man called Kelly Monteith. I thought he was so funny – we all did – and we'd squeeze in together on the sofa to watch him. Laughing in unison always made it funnier still. By now I was in the sixth form, and I'd been chosen by June, as Head of House – quite the honour – where you were looked up to by the other girls like a sort of captain of the ship, chosen for leadership qualities, for being responsible. Yes, that was me. I had the Head of House room – my own bedroom and study – and the privilege of being offered the best seat for viewing the television.

There we were laughing away so engaged with Kelly Monteith, that none of us noticed June leaning over the sofa from behind us.

"What are you all watching that's so funny?" She suddenly said, gushing her bad breath all over us.

"Kelly Monteith," I replied.

"Who? What did you say?" She hadn't got the name.

"*Kelly Monteith!*" repeated Kate Chapman, more clearly, sitting beside me.

At this, June burst out laughing. I mean she was really laughing, like his name was funnier still than his stand up show. More bad breath!

"I thought you said, 'Clean your teeth!'"

CHAPTER SEVEN

When I was sixteen, I fell in love for the first time. Finn brought home a boy from school. James. He lived near us and they were to study together.

We wrote letters to each other madly, I from my private little 'Head of House' study room in Dorset, he from his school in London. We saw each other very little but the communications sustained us. When I finished school, I spent a year working before I started university. For six months in Switzerland I was an au-pair. The other six I spent in London doing whatever jobs I could find and living on the top floor of a house of friends of my parents. These friends – Fiona and Alastair – were a good deal younger than my parents. Now I was free to see James as much as I wanted. We were both in London.

While I was trying to find my way through my emotional maze with James, Fiona used to spend hours giving me pep talks on the ways of the heart and, more fascinating still, the body. Sitting in her kitchen she'd bum cigarette after cigarette from me, and we would smoke our way through everything I needed to know about sex and love. I adored her and wished I could have a mother like her – Shelagh seemed so stuffy beside her with her attitudes on marriage and sex and a girl's virginity. For a few months, I was the daughter Fiona so wished to have had (she had two boys) and she, the young and cool mother I so wished to have had. She became my mother-friend.

With Shelagh on the other hand, I could never talk to her about these things. Conversations were awkward. Now, about the same age as she had been when she had misjudged Nat so badly, I was home again and found myself standing with her in her art room – she loved painting and was good enough for a few commissioned portraits – with a table full of artists' paraphernalia between us (not smoke and cigarettes), it was here that she told me her story about her honeymoon, the ship, the loneliness, and the horror of discovering the truth of what the future of her marriage held for her.

We conversed sideways, never facing each other, but both staring, fixated at the window. Outside, I saw the now so familiar garden, the striped lawn, the shrubbery with its ever revolving seasonal colours and the graceful weeping willow waving its limbs in recognition of me.

"You see, I learnt it all the hard way. God forbid you ever have to go through what I did." Her voice was tight. No tears. She paused at the end of her tragic tale.

"What did you feel towards him when you decided to marry him? I mean were you in love with him?"

"Well," she shrugged, "yes, the stupid thing was that I thought I was! How naive could I have been? I thought I was really in love with him. Can you believe it? He was such a gentleman, and don't forget he was very good looking."

"I don't think Dad's good looking!"

"Well you might not see it now, Darling, but he was then. And don't forget the effect of a uniform."

"Didn't you notice anything strange about him though? Perhaps he was gay? Is gay?" I had always known things weren't normal between them, but now I was finding it hard to take this in.

"Well I did yes. I mean, no, not gay – I don't think he was ever gay – just totally sexless. Asexual they call it. I don't think he even understood it himself. It wasn't something one talked about. But yes, I did notice something was different. But I liked that – his being different. He never tried to seduce me you see, and I was used to other men - all they ever did was to try *that*. I thought he was more mature. He was after all ten years older than me, my friends, other men I knew." She sighed and I saw her shoulders droop. Quite literally. "Oh goodness, if only I hadn't thought it was wedding nerves – I thought he was nervous about the wedding you see, I put it down to that. And then it was all so quick. There was no time to really know him before our wedding."

"Oh yes, right, you'd only known him six months or something?"

"Six *weeks*," she interjected, horrified herself. "Far too little time. It was now or never, and I thought that everything would change once we were married. Nothing changes just because you're married. Remember that Darling. Nothing changes."

"Didn't you tell your friends about him – the way he is? They all know we're adopted don't they? What did you used to say?"

"Oh they all assumed it was I who couldn't have children. It's the logical thing to think." There was no masking the bitterness in her reply. "I only ever told two friends the truth. Jill was one and now I can't even talk to her. He always seems to 'take her over' when she comes to stay, and I can never spend any time with her by myself. She's always busy talking together with him and not me."

"What about any of your other friends? Can't you talk to Jean, or Liz?"

"No. No I can't possibly," she said firmly. "No one knows what our marriage is really like. I couldn't tell people you see. And I can't start telling people now either. I felt sorry for him, sorry about what people would think. I couldn't betray him any more than I already had. Never say 'yes' to a man because you feel sorry for him. Or feel guilty." She made me promise that. Promise I would never ruin my life too. She would see in me her unfulfilled dreams. One day.

In 1986, just as I was getting into the swing of adult life, Shelagh discovered she had breast cancer. I was at university in London taking a B.Ed degree in Education. What I really wanted to do was be a teacher. The lump was taken out and she had radiotherapy; her doctors decided against chemotherapy.

If I could have been oblivious to the implications, my father could not have been. But I can only remember her whole ordeal being more centred on Nat's reaction to it than on Shelagh's illness. He didn't think to bring flowers to the hospital. Around her bed was emptiness compared to abundant flowers from loving husbands next to those around her. Moreover, the day she was to come out of hospital, he was shooting (it was a Saturday and he had fixed dates for this loathsome sport). Instead of sacrificing a day's shooting, he sent Finn to pick her up. At home, wanting to share her ordeal, she asked if he'd care to see her scar. He refused point blank, a clipped, hard and decisive 'no'.

She deserved better. When was it that she had not been there for him? Nat the obsessive one – obsessed with rituals and routines, obsessed with his health and bodily functions. In his dressing room was his desk – a clutter of papers and files piled high – nothing could be thrown away. Once on entering, I spied on top of his mountains of papers, his wafer-thin diaries. Year after year. Casually, I picked one up and began leafing through. On each line of each day, all that was written were times and letters like this: 06.45.BO 09.15.BWO 12.04.BNO 14.55BNO. For a long time I couldn't figure it out. Then one day the penny dropped: BO was 'bowels opened' 'W' was 'wide', and 'N' 'not'. Ah: all that time spent in the bathroom.

Nat suffered from asthma. A short time before Shelagh's cancer, I witnessed one of his asthma attacks for the first time. We were all together in London one evening, walking down the street together towards St. James' Square after a family evening out. This was a very rare occasion. It was an evening out in the West End. First, a play, 'Lettuce and Lovage,' starring Maggie Smith which they'd been wanting to see for a while. After, we dined at Wheeler's, at the time a well known fish restaurant. My father adored oysters (my mother loathed them) and this evening he could have them in abundance. It was a real treat.

As we walked back towards my father's club, for once we were all enjoying the feeling of being family, of unity, warmth. I could feel their pride in us. I felt it particularly from my mother who in turn wanted to include Nat in her joy: I saw her link her arm through his. Within seconds, he nudged her off with his elbow - a tiny flick only, but the message was contrastingly powerful. Could he not bear even this simple display of affection – this sharing? How I felt for her and grabbed her to let her know I'd got it.

Minutes later, once we'd turned into St James Square, Nat tripped on the pavement and fell. Nothing serious. He got up. But the fall brought on an asthma attack. He always thought that he was going to die when he had one, and my mother would have to coax him to believing that he could breath and that he would not die. As he stood struggling for breath people stopped to ask if we wanted an ambulance. My mother rushed off to their room to get the pills. Finn and I held him, helplessly, not knowing what to do. All I could think was how he'd done this terrible thing to my mother just before, and yet now he'd drawn all the sympathy to himself.

But now - just a few months later - it was Shealgh who was ill. It was Shealgh who had cancer, not him. It was his turn to be there for her. His inability, perhaps even diabolical refusal, to do this, astounded me.

CHAPTER EIGHT

By 1988 I had completed the teacher training degree course and went for my first interview that summer. It was a primary school in Wandsworth, London, called 'The Roche School'. It was so unlike the other three where I was invariably asked questions like: *What would I see if I came into your classroom? How would you motivate a reluctant child? How would you like to see your career develop? What can you bring to this role that other candidates may not?*

This interview was more of a chat about life. This headmistress – Carmen Roche - didn't seem to want to assess my capabilities as a future teacher at all. As I walked back down the stairs with her, she said ever so casually as if she were asking, 'If you could just close the gate on the way out, thank you,' "Well would you like the job then?" I was so taken aback I barely understood what she was saying. This was the beginning of my teaching career.

I loved my job in the Roche School. I grew as a teacher. I felt successful. On some weekends I'd go home to my parents.

"Now Missy Moo," what would you like to drink? The usual?" I was Missy Moo when we were little, and Finn was Mise – short for My Son. The names stuck forever. There we would sit, he in his armchair, and he would ask me about my teaching or what I'd been up to in London. My stories would be interrupted only by the sound of the ice cubes tinkling against the side of the glass and the crunch of crisps or nuts.

Shelagh would try to be included and interject a comment of her own. Nat, without so much as looking at her, would brush her off with a single movement of his hand, just like the flick of his elbow, an insult hanging naked in the air. Then tears, or a slammed door and my father would usually have to go to her to sooth the sting of yet another undeserved slap.

While Shelagh was forever hurting - increasingly drawing me to her need as well - Nat, on the other hand, could be charming. Never would he walk through a door before me, but make sure he held it open for me to walk through first. Always he would open the car door for me before getting in himself. He would do the same for Shelagh, for Gran, for any female. He knew how to flatter women. Perhaps he had flattered Shelagh a long time ago. He was in fact a great admirer of beautiful women. Greta Garbo was the greatest beauty of all time. He would talk of what defined a good pair of female legs. "Upturned champagne bottles," he would say, "that's the shape of elegant legs, neat thin ankles." And then he'd compliment me for having a nice figure, for being slim and for having straight teeth.

"Wait there! Don't move." Off he rushed when I was all dressed up in a taffeta ball gown, ready to go out to a fancy party. He came back with his camera, a box camera which he had exchanged a packet of Woodbine cigarettes during the war, with its brown leather case.

"Watch the birdy!" I still have his album, an album of full of Finn and me; all of them stunning pictures. Leather bound.

When I was in my twenties, he picked out a velvet hat with a floppy brim, the colour of burgundy. It was gorgeous. He told me I was the only person who could wear it, in fact that I could wear any hat and it would always look fetching. That was Nat's sort of word –'fetching'. He wanted me to try it on and then smiled at me approvingly. On rare occasions he'd present me with a gift - once it was a gift-wrapped bottle of Channel No. 5 scent. "This is the one to get I believe," were the words he used as he handed it to me without ceremony. Quite romantic really.

You must always buy expensive shoes. And you must always tip well, were pieces of Nat advice. It was Nat, not Shelagh, who took me shopping when I was eighteen to buy my first pair of evening shoes. Lovely court shoes with heels. I loved them and they lasted forever.

"Well Missy Moo, are you happy?"

"Well yes! Yes I *am* happy," I said.

"How wonderful to be happy," he replied.

May 1989. We were seated all four of us around the kitchen table, I with my back to the main window which faced the rose garden and the bird table, my mother nearest the cooker, each in our set positions. Nat had poured the wine (he would always leave it on the side and get up to refill our glasses) and he was telling us about the man who had come to door and how it had annoyed him so.

"I don't like strangers coming to the door and ringing - asking directions. And when they use our entrance as a turning place, I can't stand it. I send them away!" I had seen his hostile expression, his hostile words many a time.

"But Dad, these are just people like you and me. I mean, what is it, do you think, that makes you feel so hostile towards them?" I replied.

He turned on me like a dog biting you unexpectedly when you were only trying to stroke it.

"You sound like one of those bloody women on the BBC!" He yelled at me, fury in his every word. He might just as well have given me a slap around the cheek.

CHAPTER NINE

While I carried on at the Roche School, although life was satisfying, fun, there was a question rattling in my head that wouldn't go away: is there more to life than being a primary school teacher? And then: if I stay here, will I find myself in ten years time; doing exactly the same thing, filling my day in the same way, week in week out, year after year?

On impulse I decided to pack up my London life and my family life, and move away. I would travel. I would do something. I would return after a year, hopefully somewhat enlightened, enriched. On my return, I could consider a career move. Having become fascinated in the classroom by the different ways children learn to read, I also became fascinated with the art of story making and what it was that could captivate a child so. I had the idea that I might like to work in publishing – in children's literature. This is what I would work towards on my return.

One of the teachers in the school was a mother of twins I had in my class. She was Italian and her name was Lalli. She was beautiful, energetic and intelligent. We became friends and in the summer that year she invited me down to Italy, to the Ligurian coast where she came from.

It was this particular holiday that triggered my decision to go to Italy. I fell in love with it. Everything about Italy enticed me, particularly the language - words rolling off tongues, emphatic, tumbling one into another, bursting with meaning, yet unfathomable to me. How I wished I could speak it too – just like they did. What a dream it would be to be able to do so. Yes, I would go to Italy where I would learn to speak Italian.

One problem was money. If I wanted to stay there for any length of time, obviously I would have to find a job, and the most likely work for me to find would be teaching English. But I knew I couldn't do this without doing a TEFL course (Teaching English as a Foreign Language), so while still in London, twice a week I went to TEFL classes in the evenings, and continued my regular teaching job during the day.

In the 'classified' section of The Times, I found Italian lessons for foreigners being offered in the university town of Perugia, Umbria. I sent off for further information, filled in forms, paid a month's fees and for some cheap accommodation offered by the university. But now I realized I'd need to save up a lot more money – my salary wouldn't cover all of this – if I was serious about staying there. There was still my flight to pay for, my last month's rent in London, and of course enough money to live on for a few months before I found work. My goal was to put aside £1000 – no easy task. Any spare time I had, I waitressed or did private tutoring, but the way I really managed to make the money was by organizing a 'Workshop Week' (crafts, art, drama and music) for children, after term had finished and just before Christmas. I rented a hall in Chelsea, and took twenty children a day and charged £15 a head. It was a huge success. My outgoing expenses were fairly low and my profit was high.

I went home for the last time taking with me all my belongings including my car, which I left there for Finn to use. Shelagh hugged me tight and I knew she would miss me. A lot. Perhaps I was fleeing them.

So it was in April 1992, with a one-way ticket to Rome, one large suitcase, and £850 in travellers' cheques in a secret pocket, I left. This is how my new life all began.

During my one-month spell in Perugia, I telephoned Finn. This meant saving up enough coins and then finding a public telephone box where I could dial the number and one by one, deposit all the coins in the slot.

"Cat – I've decided to drive your car down to you!"

"What?" It was a crackly line.

"You can have your car there in Italy. You'll need it. I'm driving it down at the end of the month to Perugia for you! What's your address?"

"Really?" I was astonished. I didn't even really know where exactly I would be going after my course finished. I knew it was north and west, and somewhere around the place I'd been on holiday. I had met Paolo, a friend of Lalli's and he'd been in touch while I was making my travel plans. He had found me a job. I was to telephone. That's all I knew.

As I listened to my brother through the static, I felt suddenly afraid of driving my car alone, *and on the 'wrong' side of the road*, to an unknown destination. A train would be easier. At the same time I knew that it would be good maybe necessary, to have my car and that I should overcome the fear. "Well thanks! Yes," and gave him my address.

"OK, well I'll find it. I'll be there on Saturday. Probably around 12. OK?"

"Great! Thanks. See you then."

And so it was Finn arrived and I had my car. We drove up to Milan together, where he caught a flight back to England.

Now I faced the task of finding a place called Chiavari somewhere on the coast below Genoa. I felt more frightened now than when I left with my one way ticket from Heathrow. I had no map, GPS certainly didn't exist, nor cell phones. I felt very alone.

"Follow signs for Livorno and come off at Chiavari!" I'd managed to make the phone call to Paolo before leaving Perugia. To this day I still wonder how I managed that journey. I remember following the autostrada signs for Livorno as he'd instructed, and feeling thankful that he'd thrown that name Livorno, in at the last moment, because I really wouldn't have known. Eventually, some two hours later, I saw a sign for Chiavari. I came off, and my instinct told me to follow the black circle sign. I had absolutely no idea where I was. I parked, found another phone box, and called Paolo again. "I think I'm in Chiavari. There's a green sign on a building which says 'Hotel

Del'Orto'. Little did I know that the name, Del'Orto – of the garden – would forecast my destiny.

"I'll be there in ten minutes."

I had arrived.

Paolo had found me an au-pair position – that was 'the job' and not exactly what I'd envisaged, but it would suffice for the time being, especially as my money was dwindling fast. The new family had a lovely house above Genoa overlooking the sea, and they were very friendly and kind. They showed me to my room at the top of the house. There was a shower cubicle inside the attic bedroom, and a separate bathroom all to myself. All I needed.

Marco Bologna, the father, was very quietly intellectual, never saying an awful lot, but when he did, it was usually something interesting. He and his wife Marta, proud of their language and culture, were instrumental in my early learning of it.

Once I asked how one said, 'Leap Year' in Italian. They told me the word was 'Bisestile'. What a strange word – it didn't sound like anything meaning jumping. Marco told me that it was a Roman invention - they already knew that an extra day every four years was needed in order to synchronize the seasons. With three hundred and sixty five days *and* six hours to every year, in four years, we would have one whole day more, and in a hundred years, we would be twenty-four days out of sync. Under Julius Caesar the extra day was ostensibly squeezed in between 22nd and 23rd February, February having been until then, the *last* month of the year. March was the first month of the year. In this way there were two 23rd February. The Romans counted the date backwards – the last day - 28th - would be 1st, 27th -2nd, 26th – 3rd and so on. Therefore, this extra 23rd February was called twice 6th – bi-sextus in Latin, which in modern Italian translates into 'bisestile'.

After about a month, I met Lalli's brother Giacomo, whom I'd met on the holiday He invited me out with a group of friends.

I found myself with about fifteen of them in a little 'trattoria' out in the hills near Chiavari. Down the other end of the table, but on the opposite side to me, was a noticeably handsome young man with a gorgeous smile. His name was Lorenzo.

Someone said that this Lorenzo, had a little farm and we were all going to take a look after dinner. It was nearby. The new farm consisted of a patch of terraced land which we couldn't see because it was dark, and there was a house. We were shown inside. The place he had rented with a friend so that they could grow organic Borlotti beans and sell them. I can't say I was particularly impressed – it all looked very rudimentary and messy - and I wondered what the fuss was about. I never spoke with him, either at the dinner or during the tour, but then he would hardly be interested in a girl like me. I knew nothing about him at all. I didn't even know that the man next to me at dinner was his brother. Impossible it would have been then, to think that all because of this farmer, Lorenzo, I would abandon all my intentions.

Less than a month later, I found myself sitting on the back of Lorenzo's motorbike. It was a Yamaha 550, not terribly comfortable and with nothing to hold onto except for him. I had never been on a motorbike before, least of all somewhere in the Mediterranean on a warm summer's evening on a first date. I was twenty-six. He twenty-five. There I was in my English floral dress. I held on in awe. He was tanned and so *Italian.* He wore linen trousers and his soft cotton summer shirt billowed out with the wind. The road rushed away under my feet, and the sea looked more turquoise than ever. Green hills dotted with olive trees the other side, and every part, fixed itself in my mind as markers of the moment. He took me to a simple bar and we sat outside in the evening light almost on the sand itself, looking out onto a harbour called 'La Baia di Silenzio' drinking something fizzy. He looked at me with his soft brown eyes, and I thought I'd died   and   gone   to   heaven.

CHAPTER TEN

"I'll never get there – Italian is so complicated!" I said to Paolo. At least he spoke English. Lorenzo didn't. It really was hard. It was one thing to listen to all those lovely long sounding words with lots of s's and rolling r's but another to understand them, and more still, to be able to connect them together and say them myself. This way, the language didn't seem nearly so romantic.

"But all languages are like that," he pointed out. "They all sound great. If learning a language were easy, then everybody would speak a new one just like that. We'd all speak a multitude of languages." Yes of course.

The high I was on with Lorenzo contrasted dramatically with the difficulties of living in a new country. There was nobody to translate anything – the Bolognas didn't speak English. It was indeed quite amazing how few people spoke English. Some of the country people living around where Lorenzo had his little piece of land only spoke the Genovese dialect, so even proper Italian to their ears was alien. While Lorenzo's not speaking English forced me to make progress in Italian, I found it all very frustrating. My rudimentary Italian was not enough to express myself in the way that I would have liked.

So there was a peculiar loneliness in those early months, even when surrounded by Lorenzo's friends or family. It was all very well when I was communicating one to one, but once they were speaking amongst themselves, it went too fast. The worst would be when they started joking and laughing, at which point, I'd give up, and lose myself in my own thoughts.

Then there were cultural differences. Lorenzo had not left home. Italians don't. They tend to carry on living at home, some ad infinitum, with everything conveniently supplied and done for them.   Independence is not part of the agenda of becoming a young adult.

Lorenzo was still living at home in Chiavari while growing Borlotti beans on the patch of land with the little farmhouse. He never actually lived in the farmhouse. I lived with the Bolognas in Genoa half an hour away. The Borlotti beans, anyway, were more of an experiment than serious work. He wasn't earning any money, and was also considering going back to Milan to finish his degree in 'Agraria'.

Lorenzo's father had died ten years before and his mother, now on her own, stood very much in the middle of our relationship. Yes she made me feel welcome, but I soon discovered that I could never spend any time on my own with him. It was such a change from London where weekends were my own. Here we were expected to be with her. If we went out, she would come too – the three of us. Lorenzo's lack of independence from her and, more crucially, her distinct need for this, felt strange, and soon it began to grate. Saying 'no' to her would be a hard option. But for Lorenzo it was a way of life. For all my romantic notions about Italy, the Italian language and an Italian boyfriend to boot, this was the reality. I wasn't in England. This was another culture and I knew that *I* was the one who needed to adapt.

The Micelis were and still are a very united family. Eugenio, a vet, is the eldest, then there is Marco the artist, followed by the only daughter Monica - also an artist. Even if I felt a certain friction with their interfering mother Anna, it was she who brought them all together, and there was no other place that they were all so much in their element as home. There was always a lot of laughter. Often it was about my Italian. But this was warm and affectionate. They treated me as one of them. If I was important to Lorenzo, then I was important to them. This felt good. It felt right. I was used to a family where new people brought home were treated almost with suspicion. There seemed no such suspicion in the Miceli household. Lorenzo's mother, even if meddling, was thoughtful, generous and loving. She was consistently there, a strong point of reference for her children, but also for me. Over the years she and I have developed a close, honest and loving relationship. She is indeed very dear to me.

Also new to me, was how Italian lifestyles and work, were closely linked to our planet's forces and natural cycles. Of course in England, the weather is famous for being so atrocious and its people are robbed year in year out of anything that they can really call summer, where days roll into months and months into years with less heed paid to the season. In Italy, summer, with its soaring temperatures and perfect blue skies, is truly celebrated. Families spend most of the time together, either at the sea or walking in the mountains. Autumn is a time for family goodbyes and starting afresh with work - you get asked, *'hai fatto il cambio del armadio?'* – 'have you done the changeover in your wardrobe?' Children to go back to school to study, and study hard. The seasonal rhythms are reflected also in the kitchen: one wouldn't dream of looking for and eating a tomato in December. Artichokes in January, 'Fava' beans in May, mushrooms and chestnuts and walnuts in October, pumpkin for November, oranges in winter. All of Italy engages with the seasons, giving purpose to time and place and the people are connected through a subtle antenna of this knowledge, tying them firmly to their own land and culture.

There was so much to absorb, so much to learn. And much to enjoy too. My relationship with Lorenzo was different from any I'd had before. Not for his being Italian so much - rather just him. He was rooted. He was uncomplicated, honest, humble. I could tell him things I would tell no one else. I told him about my parents. This sense of trust was new to me. Then too, it was unusual to be with someone confidently finding his contentment working with nature, the land. I loved this in him.

I had to tell myself that he was real. *It* was real. I'd found him and, even more incredible, it was real that he could love me too.

But love doesn't resolve everything.

As the summer continued I felt more, not less, disorientated. The reason for being in Italy had changed completely and almost without my noticing. Up until now my spell in Italy was a means to an end, where enjoying its culture and language was a glorified pay-your-own-way holiday, and after, I would simply go home again, hopefully enriched. Now the strings of my neat little package were coming untied.

Living in Genoa with the Bolognas began to grate. I was after all a guest in their home. I would have to ask to make a phone call, ask if I could go out, ask if I could watch TV, ask if she needed any help. I never felt at liberty to make my own choices, be it what I ate and when, or what time I got up, went out. All the while, most of my day was spent with their children. The monotony tugged at me from one morning until the next.

Mercifully with my Peugeot 205 I had the means to go out some evenings, and drive down the coast to Chiavari, which took half an hour, and be with Lorenzo.

I desperately needed to find a proper job and proper accommodation. Being an au pair paid me all of 40,000 lire a week (€20). The main problem for finding a real job was that I had come at completely the wrong time of year. I'd arrived in May just when language schools and courses would be winding down to the end of the school year. Job-hunting would have to wait until after the summer. As for accommodation, since young Italians didn't leave home like we did, the term 'roommates' or 'flatmates' didn't exist – you shared only with your partner. To rent alone was way beyond my means.

So there I was with no job, no place of my own to live, and no money left. I started to consider packing it all in and going back to the safety of my own country and yet, here I'd found the man of my dreams. That limbic state was scary. On a practical level Lorenzo couldn't rescue me. Neither of our situations was ideal. The difference between them though, was that for Lorenzo there was of course no urgent need to change his – he wasn't floating in the way that I was - and so if anything was to alter, it was me, or at any rate, my situation. With plenty of his own decisions to make, Lorenzo, although understanding, was oblivious to my growing sense of insecurity even though I must have seemed so purposeful and strong, full of energy and unlimited resources - a far cry from what I was actually feeling.

CHAPTER ELEVEN

In September I copied a list from the Genoa telephone book of all the language schools in the city. One afternoon, armed with my TEFL certificate, I took it upon myself to go to each one asking if they needed an English teacher. After visiting five or six, only to be told they were already well equipped with teachers, I had my spiel down to a fine art. Then, by some miracle - for this is what it felt like - the last school on my list, Inlingua, was in fact looking for a new teacher. I got an interview. Several other desperate people were waiting in the corridor. My turn at last. I went into the office and a severe looking woman, called Eileen, fired off her first question, "So what do think is the best method of teaching a foreign language?"

Method? I hadn't a clue! What on earth did *I* know. I grabbed at one expression that I remembered had been used a lot at the course: 'Direct Method Teaching'. I hadn't a clue of what that really involved.

"Well, I feel that teaching people using a direct method is the most successful approach." I said with conviction.

It was a winner. I got the job.

I had to do yet another course to learn this famous 'Direct Method' - the Inlingua method. Five of us sat around a table while a now less stern Eileen gave us a lesson in Russian. We had to understand what it felt like as a *total* beginner. It was refreshing and stimulating for me - my studies at university came back about language acquisition -Teaching English the Inlingua way was about applying the same method a child uses, when he starts to acquire language. He hears the words, the phrases, over and over until one day, he starts saying them back. The students would hear the questions, the answers, and be asked to repeat back. The teacher would build the words, the sentences, the dialogues, like building bricks, and the so English language would be taught. Books, reading, and learning grammatical rules were very much second place. Inlingua is in fact the only language school that I know of that uses this method.

With my newly found self-confidence, I was ready to begin teaching. Equipped with two huge brief cases of 'Inlingua' books, and an address in a factory in a remote village forty minutes from Chiavari, I set off in my Peugeot. I found my way there in the dark, as their course was after business hours, and was met by five extremely nice Italians, receptive and sensitive and ready to hang onto my every word.

Once I'd started working, the balance of vulnerability and security shifted. Staying in Italy, certainly for the foreseeable future, became viable. I only had to find a place to live. Here too I was lucky. Lalli's younger brother Giacomo needed to find accommodation too. There was an apartment which belonged to an elderly aunt available at a nice affordable 'family rate'. Giacomo and I quickly developed a bond, and with Lorenzo near at hand (in fact he was practically living there too), at last I felt a deeper sense of stability and belonging.

During the day, 'Inlingua' also sent me to an all male secondary school. Little did I know what I was letting myself in for here though. Rather than five polite and eager-to-learn Italian adults male *and* female, I had classes of twenty-five adolescents, *all* boys, with no interest in learning English at all. All the other teachers were male. This was because the school was not the regular high school, but rather a specialist school, training boys to become car mechanics, carpenters, electricians, plumbers or metal solderers. It had been decided that year, 1992, that two hours of English per week for each class would be an important part of the curriculum. Being young, female and English, coupled with the fact that my Italian was probably quite funny to listen to (perhaps endearing), made my whole presence rather a novelty, and not only to the boys, but to the staff as well. I didn't want to be endearing. Or funny. Or so noticeable. I wanted to teach and be understood. But this was a difficult task, actually nearer to impossible. The two hour lessons seemed interminable. I think it was a waste of money and time for the school – while the boys seemed to be paying a fair amount of attention to *me,* I know that very few paid any attention to the actual English language. I dreaded walking in through the front gate each day, but I stuck it out for a whole school year. Probably what they call a 'character building' life experience.

Inlingua paid really poorly – I earned 12,000 Lire per hour (€6). It would have been impossible to live on this alone, but as time moved on, I met more people and started to give private lessons earning nearly three times as much. Later I got a job as art teacher at the American International School continuing with the individual English lessons in my spare time. Lorenzo decided to stay in Chiavari instead of going back to university in Milan, for which I felt thankful.

Over the next couple of years, he took on other pieces of land, and started market gardening seriously, from which he hoped to make a living. He was also growing the vegetables organically. Yes this *would* yield a greater profit, but Lorenzo felt very strongly about not using chemicals on the land. And like his late father, he had a passion for farming. He used greenhouses so that his produce – potatoes, tomatoes, zucchini, aubergines, lettuce and basil - could be available early and late in the season, and therefore he could sell at a considerably higher price. Basil has been a native plant of Liguria for centuries, growing well with that particular climate and sea air, so it is no surprise that the now famous pesto sauce comes specifically from the cuisine of Liguria. I used to help Lorenzo bunch up five mini basil plants into newspaper and tie each up with an elastic band. He would sell each bunch for 500 Lire – the equivalent of 25 cents in euros. At one point I suggested I take a mix of fresh vegetables to the school and see if I could sell some there. So I filled my car with crates of vegetables and straight away sold all the crates. The vegetables became popular and I began taking orders.

In the winter he produced olive oil. Organic or course. This too was highly prized because Lorenzo handpicked his olives. The old Ligurian method was to leave the trees unpruned. The branches thus being so high, the only way to harvest them was to let the olives drop to the ground. Left on the ground, they would be overripe and acidic.

Being with Lorenzo I learned all about olive oil, from tree, to olive, to 'frantoio', to 'Extra Virgin'. I always thought that 'Extra Virgin' meant first pressing. It did in the 'old days' when olives were literally pressed by a rotating stone driven by a donkey. Now, olives are taken to the 'frantoio', where they are made into pulp, stones and all, by vicious looking round blades and then filtered through a mechanical system where eventually the water is extracted by means of a centrifuge. At the very end of this process, comes a stream of beautiful bright green, pure, exquisite smelling olive oil. Extra Virgin simply means that the oil is mechanically obtained and not chemically. Thus there is no alteration in its substance and its natural acidity does not exceed 0.8%. In order to have such low acidity, the olives need to be top quality and freshly picked, usually when they are green just turning brown, long before they become completely black. Before I'd thought that a black olive was a different variety, but they're just overripe, or at any rate, overripe for Extra Virgin olive oil.

I was now an Italian pouring lashings of olive oil on everything I ate. The aroma and the taste right after the oil comes back from the 'frantoio' almost defy the imagination - I can only describe it as almost bitterly green and earthy, filling the palette and prickling one's throat. A good new oil can make you cough. Wickedly high in calories, it's a wonderfully healthy fat, and even though it has such a strong flavour, it is what all Italian babies are weaned onto and all Italian children grow up on. Later when I had my own children to wean, I did what they do in Italy. What better than a purée of Lorenzo's organic vegetables from his beloved hills, with a dollop of his Ligurian olive oil and a tasty grating of Parmesan cheese?

By the summer of 1994, we could afford to rent a house together. This first house was tall and thin, with just three rooms. Each room was on a separate floor connected by stairs of black slate. We had an orange tree for fresh orange juice, and from our bedroom window at the top, we could see a slice of the sea. The house was painted Genovese style: yellow ochre and dirty pink, darker lines bordering the windows and edges of the walls, and had green shutters and a grey slate roof. Because slate is mined in the valleys in Liguria, slate is used everywhere there: facades of churches, paving stones, windowsills, tables, kitchen counters.

There was no hot water except for the shower, and no heating. We would light two wood burners every morning and once we'd got them going, we managed to keep ourselves warm during the few colder months. We had next to nothing in the way of furniture: a sofa-bed Lorenzo's mother didn't need, kitchen chairs picked up from a market, a table, fridge and stove luckily already there, we had one wardrobe and a round table with a beautiful alabaster set of chess on it. Lorenzo had always played chess with his father sitting at this table. We slept on the floor on the old mattress which was from the little rented farmhouse, later, Lorenzo crafted a frame and slats for it. There was one bookshelf, one television and one corner kitchen cupboard and that was it. It was perfect.

CHAPTER TWELVE

Christmas of the same year that Lorenzo and I had found our house together, I was on a visit to my parents. Sitting at my old familiar desk, I was toying with some ideas for teaching the art lessons, when my mother appeared in my bedroom doorway. I began telling her about my new job and some of the ideas.

"What do you think?"

"Well, that's no surprise you're interested in art." She said. "Your natural mother was artistic."

My genetic history had been shrouded in mystery. Until this moment. And now it just popped out, so casually. In the 1960s, indeed up until 1978, the law was that we adoptees could not have access to records; we were given only a few bare threads. We would take on our new parents' identity, which was easy because there *was* no other identity – we were '*blank slates*' to be moulded into our parents' children. Any genetic knowledge (apart from physical traits of course) was dissolved when the mothers who had given birth to us, signed the documents. They too would sever themselves from us, giving themselves a new chance in life without the hindrance of an illegitimate child. It was a win-win situation for all concerned. As far as I knew, the 'blank slate' theory worked. I liked the 'blank slate' theory. Shelagh was my 'real' mother now and I took after *her*. Whenever I told people I was adopted – along with the pity I might see in their eyes – they often would react, and indeed still do, by thinking I needed comforting. Quite often, they console me by telling me they knew So-and-so who was also adopted.

People have a habit of doing that: they think they are giving comfort by telling you about someone they know who is in the same position as you - a sort of, 'you're not alone in this', as if it's supposed to comfort. It never does – I find it more of an insult.

When I was younger, people would tell me how adoption was "special", that I was special, as if it were a privilege. Again, I couldn't understand. Not what they were saying, but rather, why they felt the need to say it. That was the whole thing: It *was* a privilege. I *was* special.

An older woman - a grandmotherly sort of older - in regard to one such situation replied to me, "my grandmother was adopted."

At the time, I thought, "So what?" And going by my friend's age, that adoption would have taken place around the mid to late 1800's, so it seemed even more out of place that this person could make such comparison. In her case, her infant grandmother was left on a rotating stone wheel at the front door of a Florence orphanage. But this wretched grandmother had nothing to do with me! My friend went on to tell me that these babies of a hundred years ago were often left with letters written by the mother, or with 'tokens', like half of a locket, or one of a pair of earrings, in the hope that there would be better circumstances one day in the future, when, by presenting one half, mother and child could be reunited. Her grandmother had a scar on her palm, she went on, and always said that her birth mother had put it there purposefully so that through this scar, she would, one day, find her.

At the time, I wasn't interested and nodded politely. All I could think was that this was what happened to unwanted babies a hundred years ago. They were abandoned – so unlike babies in my day. Now. We were cared for and given the best - this was something to be proud of, being adopted. We were special – we were *chosen*. And we were most certainly not *abandoned*!

Here I was, twenty-nine, standing there with Shelagh, and talking about my genetic origins for the first time. It would be another ten years before I was able to assimilate this word 'abandonment' into my own history when I would come to learn that the difference between the baby left by her mother in the 1800's, and me left by *my* birth mother in 1965, was absolutely nothing.

Whoever my mother was, she left me in the hands, not of an orphanage but of another institute –The Adoption Society of Knightsbridge, London. Yes, I had a birth certificate but at the time of my birth, it was against the law to be able to have it or to see it. Ever. The idea of a reunion, at that time, was out of the question. It was therefore as good as nothing; indeed its worth was far less than half a coin, or one earring.

I don't know if the mother who gave birth to me could have left me an object, a trinket, but what I do know is that, even then in 1965, while I was convinced that she had not abandoned me, convinced she had done the *'right thing'* for me, convinced too that I had almost *come from* Shelagh, I would still have treasured a trinket from her. I would very much like to have lived with that knowledge, like my friend's grandmother, that my mother still had had every intention of finding me one day.

I did however, know that she had called me Jane. It was the only piece of information I had about my birth mother. I don't know when Shelagh told me this - it was something I always knew, just like the knowing I was adopted but not being able to remember the being told part. Of course it wasn't a trinket - it wasn't anything that would lead me to her – but it was the one (and only thing) that she had given to me. A name. I held onto this fragment of information - my talisman - not tenaciously, just tenderly, until the day I found her.

So here we were, Shelagh and I, both of us standing there framed by the door, chatting about my being an art teacher, when this bolt of information was given to me, just like that, out of the blue.

Something pricked me inside.

"Oh really? Well, that doesn't have anything to do with my being art teacher. I think it's come from *you.*" I said, protecting both of us. We both knew Shelagh was artistic.

"No," she replied. " I think there's more to you that has come from elsewhere. Not from me."

"Like what?" I asked.

"Oh I don't know. There have been times when you've said something, or had a certain expression, and I've thought, ' but I haven't taught Catriona that, that's just her. Not me.' "

"Oh," was all I could think. But I was curious enough to want to carry on this conversation.

"So how do you know my mother was artistic?"

"Well, they told us."

"What? What did they tell you?"

"Well, that your natural mother was at art school when she had you. She was studying 'the arts.' "

"Art?" I queried.

"No, I believe it was a type of university specializing in all artistic subjects, acting, music, art and all those."

" Which university?"

"Well, it was in Canada."

"*Canada!!*" I exclaimed. So far away. Canada? Why there? I was astonished. "Why on earth was she in Canada?" I asked.

"Well, her family had emigrated there from England."

"So why was I born in England?"

"Well, she very much wanted you to be born in England. She wanted to come back to have you here. She also wanted you to go to private school and be brought up a Christian."

Here were the very first words I had ever heard that evoked even the tiniest idea of my birth mother as real person, one who had existed. She had had personal wishes for her baby – well apart from the name Jane of course. It was such an odd moment. There was so much to take in.

"Where in Canada was this?"

"I'm not sure I should be telling you this."

"Why not? Why can't you tell me?"

"Well alright then, it was Montreal." She told me with reluctance. "It was a private school. She came from a good family."

"But was she English? Did she come from England?"

"Yes yes. Well, I *think* so." She replied. "Yes I'm quite sure she was English."

And then, "You don't want to look for her do you?"

But it wasn't a question.

CHAPTER THIRTEEN

February 1996, Lorenzo and I decided to get married. Shelagh, thrilled, started to make arrangements and the date was set for 31st August. We would be married in England.

Back in 1992, her breast cancer had metastasized to her spine and at the time, she had had radiotherapy, and as far as we all knew, it had gone. Towards the end of 1995, I was home again for Christmas. She was driving and as I sat next to her, she suddenly said, "Oh no! Blast!"

"What? What's blast?" I replied.

"My triple vision is back again." I didn't know what she was talking about so she explained that this had recently started – that she literally was seeing triple.

It turned out a she had tiny tumour in her brain that was compressing the optic nerve hence the triple vision. During my two-week stay, she was immediately sent in for radiotherapy and I was the one who took her to hospital. Now I was alarmed.

In March the following year of 1996, just after Lorenzo and I had just decided to get married, my father was phoning me with the news that yet another tumour had been found – it had returned to her spine. But there was now something new in this situation: for the first time I could hear *concern* in his voice. It was this that troubled me.

"I'm afraid Mummy is not well at all." He explained that she was needing cortisone. Yes, cortisone – I knew the name of this drug and its association with people with cancer – people dying of cancer.

And then, "She's not as mobile as she usually is." The words hammered themselves through my ear and a sense of panic swept through me. What did they mean?

Could I come for a visit? He would pay for my ticket this time. It was a Sunday and Lorenzo and I went to the cinema that evening but I couldn't concentrate on the film, I was so overwhelmed by this ominous, very frightening piece of news.

I flew back for Easter shortly after, and we decided to make it a surprise for her. Arriving at Gatwick airport there was no one to meet me – there never was. Why they never came to meet me, I shall never know. I didn't like to ask the favour and they never offered. I would get the train, or rather three trains to be precise. But this time, each section of journey weighed so much more; dragging that old suitcase up and then down those steps at Clapham Junction to change platforms and squeeze my way through the dirty corridor of the Exeter train to Salisbury.

Eventually I arrived, and my father, there to meet me, waiting in the car outside, no longer even on the platform to greet me as he used to. Finn was home too. I went straight into the drawing room, knowing I'd find her the other side of the fireplace in her usual chair in front of the television.

"Hello Mummy!"

"Oh! Oh ! Oh!" She exclaimed. The pure delight, the surprise and utter gratitude were spilling from her. But so frail she looked, so small there, seated in the familiar armchair that now almost engulfed her. So sweet, so much love in her eyes, tinged with a sadness of a lifetime.

In those few seconds, her surroundings registered fiercely inside of me: there beside her was a Zimmer frame - cold, geriatric, clinical - clashing loudly with the antiques I was so accustomed to seeing.

We talked a little - there's always plenty to say when you've just arrived - and then it was time to help her up and get to the kitchen for some lunch.

What happened next I was not prepared for.

She couldn't get up from the chair by herself. That alone was hard to take in. Finn had to help her up. Then she leaned on her Zimmer frame and began to walk. But she wasn't walking. I stood behind her and watched her drag one leg forward, click the knee into 'lock', drag the other leg, lock that one too, drag-click-drag, ever so slowly, again and again and again covering all of a couple of metres. She still had the whole length of the room to go, and the hall.

"She can't walk! She can't walk! She can't walk!" were the words that screamed inside of me.

I edged along behind her so she could not have noticed my eyes full of tears, giving away the pain in my stomach and in my tight throat - my throat so tight and swollen - it would have been impossible to utter a word.

I'd no idea. But even if I had known, nothing could have saved me from that pain in that moment. Seeing is believing.

This lesson I learned again when I came back in June, having finished the school year at the International School. I planned to stay for three weeks to help with wedding preparations that were now underway. Shelagh was enjoying organizing everything. At last her Catriona was getting married and she could sound the trumpets to her friends. Finn had warned me her face was rather blown up because of the cortisone. I tried to imagine what Shelagh's blown up face would be like but I just couldn't summon an image.

Home once again, same journey, same train to Clapham Junction, same old heavy suitcase, same rotten old steps and same Salisbury station, and my same Dad there to pick me up.

As we neared the house ten minutes later, his words were, "I'm afraid Mum's days are numbered."

I felt a lurch in my stomach just as I had when I had heard the words *not so mobile as she usually is*. I remained silent. She was only sixty-six – for me she had years and years left.

Again I entered the house, a replay of the Easter visit as I rounded the corner in the drawing room to find her in the same chair.

Oh God. My eyes gave my mind and heart away. She spoke first.

"Yes I'm afraid I'm a bit puffy in the face. I know I look like a bullfrog."

She was unrecognizable. My mother had gone and in her place a grotesque creature. I wanted her face to come back. I wanted *her* to come back. Her beautiful soft green eyes were now slits, her chin one with her neck like someone obese, her tiny mouth suffocated by swollen cheeks.

No longer was there the pretence of walking - we helped her from chair to wheelchair with heaves and shuffles. And before lunch, it was an assisted visit to the loo.

"One, two, three, uuup!" giving her the under arm support, wheelchair foot supports up, push chair out the way, zimmer in place, shuffle shuffle, lean on Zimmer while I pulled down her underpants and trousers, "Here you are, can you feel the seat behind your knees? Ready? And down. Ok, Mum?"

"Yes thank you Darling."

I waited outside to be summoned back. Off to the kitchen. Lunch time. All this within the first half an hour of my arrival back home from Italy.

We - my father my brother and I - went to see the family doctor the next day. His first words were, "The nurses tell me they think she'll make it to the wedding, but I don't think she will."

My wedding was only two months away! I didn't understand. How could she not make it to my wedding? There had to be more time. I thought it was a question of years. How could I take this in – that we were talking about weeks?

My throat was tight again, and I couldn't say a word. I was in the middle of a nightmare and I wanted to wake up, but everything was real – the table, the walls, the examining bed, my brother and father there beside me, Dr Pelly himself.

I had seen her as immortal – perhaps we all do that. Our mothers are our eternal compass, and we are attached to them by an invisible elastic - we stretch away, we come back – we always come back to replenish ourselves with their everlasting nourishment and love. Our mothers are always there. It was therefore impossible for me to understand that mine was not going to be there forever. Sitting there at the doctor's, with three men seated gently around, I felt very alone and very frightened.

I couldn't share my emotions. Shelagh was mine – my feelings for her were precious and these men had no right to them. Not even Finn, dear Finn whose pain was as great as mine. He needed me in that moment but I couldn't hold him up. So I kept my feelings within, tucking them away in my aching heart as we walked away from the surgery and out to the car.

I stayed on all summer with my mother, the entire summer and not just the three weeks that I had planned; there was no question of not. Nat went into a depression and made life heavy, difficult, worse. The time was punctuated by Finn's weekend visits from London, and each day by the district nurses' visits to give medication or a bed-bath or by the voluntary 'carers' who came twice a day to help dress and undress her for bed. These were my moments of sanity where I could connect to the world outside.

It was no longer simply getting her on to the loo, but the 'comode'. It was no longer leaving her tactfully to it, but a helping hand was needed to finish up. No dignity left. Sometimes, she couldn't make it there on time, and there was the messy cleaning up.

On one occasion, I left her sitting in her wheelchair downstairs, asking her if she'd be all right for five minutes while I went to wash my hair.

"Help!" I heard her weak voice cry. I rushed down, and there she was crumpled on the floor in front of her chair, unable to get up.

"I've been calling and calling." She was nearly crying.

"Oh Mum, I didn't hear you, my head was up-side-down under the tap," came my desperate apology. We were both feeling desperate I think. She was crying from exasperation, and I saw how her own state was hurting her too, not just me.

My birthday came and went. No gifts from my parents but a beautiful bouquet of flowers from Lorenzo. I missed him so much. We didn't have internet then, nor messaging – I didn't have a cell phone - nor could you make cheap phone calls. It felt as if Lorenzo was part of a different world. But we were still going to get married. The wedding was going through and so much of that summer was spent involved with these preparations. It was one goal for my mother to look forward to. In fact, my presence and the impending wedding had the one wonderfully positive effect on her. She didn't suddenly get up and walk but she didn't get worse as Dr Pelly had predicted.

I stayed with her literally every waking moment of her day. If I ever went out on my own account (what freedom to just go around the supermarket, alone), I needed a very good reason, primarily for Nat, but also for her, with no holes in it. What time was I coming back? Why did I have to do that? I pushed her around the garden in the heavy chair, I showed her the plants, we talked about them and the flowers, I read to her out loud - Sebastian Fawkes 'Birdsong'. I brought her upstairs, downstairs, heaved her from wheelchair to armchair, to car seat, to Stanner stair lift, to bed, lifting her dead legs each time, puffed up her cushions, fed her, dressed her, talked to her and but above all loved her. I really loved her. She never complained.

"Yes, thank you Darling," came her reply when I asked her if she was comfortable. She just let me look after her. My moments of respite were when she'd snooze and after I'd put her to bed at 9.30pm.

I got thinner and thinner. My wedding dress kept having to be altered. But my being there made her world a different place, and that was the important thing. She deserved that. My mum was sick, I loved her and there was little time left and I wanted to be there for her.

Nat, like a child, needed the attention. He had indeed always been the 'sick one' looked after by her. This was new for him to look after someone else. He was suffering watching his wife die in front of his eyes. Poor Nat. Perhaps he too thought of her as immortal.

It was nearing the end of August now, and our wedding. I hadn't seen Lorenzo for nearly three months. My father never suggested I have a break and go and visit him. I couldn't decide this for myself as I had no money. However an old friend of the family, Joan Anderson, whom Nat respected and admired, told him that I looked far too thin and wan to be getting married and that I should be given some time off. She was very firm with him. So it was that I was allowed back 'home' to Italy for just a week where I could eat what and when I liked, wake when I liked and look after only myself. Best, was seeing Lorenzo. We took ourselves off the next day to our favourite rock in a secluded spot along the Ligurian coast, where I soaked up the warm rays of the sun that I'd so missed, and felt the sea and warmth on my skin.

Those days flew by and soon we were driving up to England together in his brother's Volkswagen Passat.

While I was away, Shelagh had a stroke. On my return I found her speech was slurred and she was saying very odd things about people and who they were and her mouth drooped on one side. That's when she was awake. Most of the time, she was in a deep slumber, almost a coma.

It seemed the end was near now – she would die in the next few days. How unfair could life be? It felt like all my endeavours to prolong her life that summer, in vain. Why did she have to be robbed right at the end? Couldn't her dream of seeing her daughter walk down the aisle and into a happy future - the one she never had - come true? Couldn't that be a parting gift?

Wish denied.

A day or two before the wedding, we had to come to a decision – do we cancel the wedding or not? Was it going to be a wedding or a funeral? It was so stressful not knowing. So we together decided that even if she died, we would go ahead with the wedding. Once this decision was made there was a sense of relief. Relatively speaking.

First thing in the morning of the day of my wedding I went to her in her room, and saw her there in her bed motionless, her face grey, her body lifeless, laid out on her back.

I went to her and bent my ear to her mouth expecting nothing – no breath.

Ever so lightly, there was. There was the faintest of breath. Still alive. Oh thank God! She wasn't dead. She wasn't dead. It was going to be ok. Everything would be fine.

She woke later, and the looking after of her was in the safe and loving hands of the wonderful nurses who I had by now got to know so well.

My father was getting himself prepared and I allowed myself to be preened and made up by two wonderful old friends, my bridesmaids. They were making a mess of my hair – I hadn't had any kind of run through and had no clue as to what kind of coiffure I should have, the blind leading the blind. On went my dress, I slipped my feet into my shoes, my earrings, and lastly my veil. But I didn't enjoy the reflection of myself in the mirror. Nothing – my face, my hair - looked right. On my way down, I looked into my mother's room to show her how I looked but I don't think she saw. My father was downstairs waiting for me. He, the nurses, the lady who'd prepared my bouquet, all had tears in their eyes as they looked at me. They were all staring and I couldn't really see why.

Sitting in the back of the Rolls Royce, all shiny and ceremonial, my father beside me, I could only feel a numbness. It seemed surreal to find so many people, gathered at the church, waiting and ready to look upon me the bride. As we drove along, I knew every curve, every hedgerow, the familiar way in which the cows dotted the meadows, with only the task of chewing grass, so perfectly oblivious to the troubled bride passing by.

"Did you check the post this morning?" I said.

"Oh, no. How silly. I forgot." The first time ever that my father had forgotten to the check the post.

On this most surreal of days, I stood at the entrance to the church. I saw very familiar faces - friends, smiling admiringly, standing in the first pew. Now the time was for me. For Lorenzo. For us. The organ burst into play, sound blocking my worries. At long last I felt myself glow inside as my father and I walked up the aisle, and faces turned to welcome me in. Beyond their warm and teary eyes, there, standing turned towards me and waiting, was my Lorenzo, so elegant, so handsome, so wonderfully loving. After all this, he was still there.

The ceremony went on, with love and warmth and meaning. Our vicar, sweet, sensitive, held us all together, Lorenzo and I, the congregation, and we rejoiced.

70

Finn stood at the front of the choir stall and sang his heart out. He had written me a letter shortly before, telling me how very proud he was to have me as his sister, and how I had managed to face things in life in a way that he had not. He wished me all the happiness in the world and that I should continue on my way, but that, come what may, he would always be there for me. He read one of the readings too. Beautifully. He looked wonderful then, so smart and distinguished in his morning coat and so confident too.

We had decided, as Shelagh was so very ill, so close to death, that after the service we would come up to her room for a quiet blessing. There would be myself and Lorenzo, Nat and Lorenzo's mother, Anna, and Finn.

As we stood around her bed we all wondered how much she was really taking in, I laid my bouquet on the bed beside her while the vicar said a blessing. Her eyes glistened. I looked across the bed at Finn, and his were brimming with tears. He raised them towards me, begging. My heart tumbled and my stomach lurched and I had to draw mine away immediately in fear of the pain.

But our wedding was wonderful. I loved every moment. I loved the music, the prayers, the readings, the address, our vows to one another, and the blessing. The blessing with my beloved Shelagh – so much love surrounding us all – and our reception after in our beautiful garden; what better place? I loved our departure with our friend Alistair standing on the road in front of our barn, spontaneously playing his bagpipes, as we drove off in the old Passat. We were smiling, we were involved in our own story now, and we had so many friends sharing it with us.

CHAPTER FOURTEEN

Shelagh didn't die then. She went on to live for another nine months. Christmas and Easter came and went. So did I. I became pregnant, and it was my joy of all joys. I told her on Easter day but found her disappointingly unenthusiastic. I felt a little robbed. She was given spells in the palliative care unit in Salisbury District Hospital and I went back to help with the transitions back home, learning how to operate a contraption rather like a miniature crane to hoist her in and out of bed. I had the task of looking for a carer, as Nat was incapacitated with depression. I found Angela. Angela moved in. Although Shelagh had deteriorated further, for me nothing was as hard ever again. I didn't live there any more, or for that matter ever again, but came back and forth as much as possible now that my father paid for my trips.

I still believed in miracles. I still believed my mother, my very own mother, would never die. But one day in June, I got a phone call from Nat. She had gone into a coma. I bought tickets on the next flight out of Genoa on June 6th 1997, which was the next day, but he called again at 6am that morning, to tell me that she'd passed away during the night. Lorenzo heard me speak on the telephone, and as I moved back into the bedroom, he was already holding open his side of the quilt for me to climb into, and I let myself be enfolded completely by his warm, strong, safe body, and I wept silent tears.

This time Lorenzo was accompanying me home. When we arrived, there were the funeral people already there sitting in the kitchen over a cup of tea, chatting politely with my father and Finn, and waiting for me to see her before taking her body away. I had no desire to go and see her. I would have done anything to avoid looking at her in her death state. But I found that it was expected and I couldn't say no. Lorenzo accompanied me as I eased my way unwillingly into her bedroom in dread of the sight of her body and what effect it would have upon me. I had never seen a dead person in the flesh before, and certainly not someone I had loved. I found it shocking and hideous. I kept my distance in fear of her deadness that lay before me. I couldn't go any closer, let alone touch her stone cold body. Her mouth was open. Why hadn't anybody closed her mouth? No tears. I had shed them a long time ago.

The cremation, even though done in the "best taste", I found unbearable, watching the coffin go slowly down knowing it was about to be eaten up by a roaring furnace. I kept all the pain in, just as I had at the Dr Pelly's surgery, refusing to allow Nat or Finn see it. In contrast, the memorial service was a consolation, as moving as our wedding had been. The same church was packed with people almost spilling out of the door, it was wonderful to feel such love. The horror of her dying was over.

At this time we moved into our second house. It was better situated, but didn't have any heating either. We fixed up electrical heaters upstairs and the same old wood burner down. Rent was cheap and the view from upstairs was gorgeous. The house with its large terrace overlooked the sea and the promontory of Portofino that was silhouetted by the setting sun every evening.

Poor financially, rich in so many other ways. While pregnant I gave up my job at the American International School, and we managed to make ends meet with Lorenzo's vegetables and olive oil, and a few reduced hours of my teaching.

Camilla was born at the end of that same year. She was born in England. I had so wanted that. While I was pregnant with her, I carried a deep sadness over the death of Shelagh, whom I so missed and needed now. I wanted her to be there for me while I too became a mother. I had my mother-in-law, but of course it wasn't the same thing. I didn't want to be told how to do things, I didn't want her help – she was the wrong person, the wrong mother – and besides, she did things differently. I felt as though she would be absorbing my baby under the umbrella of *her* family, without really seeing me. With Shelagh gone my mother-in-law would take over, filling a space that didn't belong to her, and that felt unfair.

I had no genetic history - and just now I felt the absence of that strongly. Bringing my own baby in to the world would give *me* a sense of place and belonging.

The need, therefore, to hold my own was great. *I* would decide where and how she would be born, and *I* would decide how I would look after her. This baby was mine; my genes connected her to me. I had to go to England to have her.

But it wasn't just about identity and getting away from my mother-in-law. There was another reason that I was so determined. I believed that the care offered in England was better. In Italy, pain relief for giving birth doesn't really exist. It is quite amazing. Nothing is offered to take the edge off - they've never heard of 'gas & air', or the 'TENS' gadget, or pethadine, and epidurals are offered in a very few hospitals as pain relief, then, only with a series of signatures and certificates well before the birth. It would be unheard of to offer a mother starting her labour, a nice warm bath there in the labour ward. While you would plan *where* to have your baby, the *how* would not be on the agenda for anti-natal care. It didn't seem that there was any such thing as a 'home birth'. In Genoa where Camilla might have been born, at that time, they deemed it necessary to shave women and have them lying on their backs with their feet in stirrups. The doctor has to be in a good position – forget what the mother needs. A gynaecologist has to be present at the birth even though it will be an 'ostetrica' (equivalent of a mid-wife) who will do most of the assisting. But it will have to be the gynaecologist who will do the stitches after, if necessary, not the mid-wife as in England. I had been particularly horrified that stitches administered after the birth would be given without any local anaesthetic.

Many say all this derives from the strong influence of the Catholic Church - that the woman has always suffered and must continue to do so. Perhaps this theory is a little far-fetched, but some believe that as so many of the medics involved are men (my gynaecologist was a man), they have no tangible understanding of the real pain that women suffer in child-birth. Furthermore, I think it's because Italy and Italians simply don't keep up with the times in many practical aspects of life - they just carry on like they did in the 1800s.

Perhaps I was wrong, but I was afraid. I wanted TENS, I wanted gas & air, I'd have a shot of pethadine, and I rather liked the option of an epidural too! And please, I would definitely want a local anaesthetic for the stitches. I had no idea if it would be a long birth – there was no precedent to go by without knowing my birth mother. Although Shelagh might not really have been so much help over the birth itself, she would have offered familiar solace during this venture into unknown territory. It was years later that I would discover an alternative that Italy does offer: wonderful warm birthing baths. But for now, clinging to England felt like my best option.

My instincts told me that I would be in for a long and gruesome labour and birth. Long it was. Gruesome no. I had that epidural so that Camilla came into the world with me smiling all the way, at 8.30pm Friday 5th December 1997. The care was supreme. My baby was perfect. My little miracle. Lorenzo had been with me the whole way. He had even cut the umbilical cord himself. We came home two days later with our little bundle.

Home in England was cosy and warm. Although Nat went into a depression yet again the moment I came out of hospital, it still felt good to be there. We were independent of anybody telling us how or what to do. We had our own bathroom with the spare room, and I remember enjoying a bath together, Lorenzo and I, holding our little tiny Camilla too - all three of us in the warm water together. It was very special. We were now a family.

Camilla was just twelve days old when we flew back to Italy. Back in the new house we'd moved into, Lorenzo would get up in the summer at 4.30am every day to pick his courgettes. Given the markets wanted the flowers of the courgettes to still be *open*, and because they'd start to close up with the heat of the day, it was necessary to pick them at first light. A courgette that still has its lush crisp yellow flower is the sign that it has only just been picked. It was essential that Lorenzo's courgettes looked enticing. A fresh courgette flower dipped in a batter and quickly fried is delicious. Later he would have a quick lunch with me, and then a snooze, after which I would come up to gently wake him with a 'café sciaccherato' (a cocktail he loved, of an expresso, sugar, and ice, shaken up to a froth and filtered into a glass). Then he'd be on his way again and not back until t least 8pm. He didn't really see a great deal of Camilla.

Two years later, at the beginning of the new millennium, everything changed. Our sister in law Elena, married to Lorenzo's eldest brother Eugenio, made us a proposal.

This entailed a move from Liguria to Tuscany. As beautiful as Liguria is, with its Riviera coastline, stunning sea views and neatly painted tall houses in secret little harbours, working the land is a labour of love. The Ligurian Apennine Mountains simply go straight down into the sea leaving little space to cultivate crops. Olive trees grow on terraces built centuries before, and Lorenzo spent more time organizing the nets under the trees to run down the various levels, than actually picking olives. Tuscany on the other hand, offers wide-open spaces of fertile land set between those famous dreamy rolling hills. A farm, with vineyards and olive groves with ancient Tuscan buildings to invite travellers, was the undertaking Elena had in mind for us to manage. An *Agriturismo.*

When we first met, Lorenzo said that his dream was to have a farm either in Africa or in Tuscany. He was connected to Africa having lived there as a small child. His father, born in the Italian colony of Libya, had a large estate there and a successful import-export business. The Micelis lost everything with Kaddafi's 'coup d'état' in 1969. When they moved back to Italy, they chose Genoa because it was near Chiavari where

Lorenzo's mother came from. His father at the time had wanted to buy a farm in Tuscany, but it would have been too far to try and manage from Genoa (it's about a two and a half hour drive). Instead they bought one closer, in Piedmont. Sadly Mario, his father, to whom Lorenzo was particularly connected, died when Lorenzo was only sixteen, and they sold the farm.

Some twenty years later, Lorenzo was being offered the opportunity to realize his father's dream. And his own too. Moving to a farm in Tuscany would be closing the door on the type of hard labour that he was used to, and it would open a whole new world: wine. Instead of vegetables, precious vines. He would cultivate these plants year round. What greater satisfaction, than to see a year's work transformed into something so noble as a bottle of wine, his very own?

For my part, I was sceptical when Elena said she thought she'd found 'just the thing'. I was pregnant with our second child, Tom, so it didn't feel like the right time for another big change. Not that I feared change. I was certainly used to that; and I didn't doubt that the venture could succeed. What I doubted was my own capabilities. There were nine apartments located in the two old stone farmhouses. Part of our income would be made from filling these for at least six months of the year. An *agriturismo* is a lot to manage and there was a daunting amount to learn. I was only a teacher after all - that was all I knew how to do. I didn't even know how to switch on a computer, let alone make documents and files and spread sheets. I knew nothing of creating a website, marketing, working with agencies, contracts and policies, bookings and cancellations, fiscal codes, invoices, taxations, ledgers, keeping the balance. Italy is famous for requiring licences for every little, or big, enterprise. Lorenzo was already a certified farmer but I would have to take an Italian exam in order to have the authorization to be the titleholder of my side of the business. For him, he was merely climbing up his own ladder but for me it was something totally alien. For the exam I would have to study basic accounting, catering, tourism, legislation and commerce. All this would of course be in Italian.

Elena though, believed I could do it. So I knuckled down to studying throughout the latter half of my pregnancy and I passed the exam. I became the titleholder of my side of the business and the apartments were under my name. The land and winery were under Lorenzo's. The scope of the new business was enormous. In the freezing month of February 2000, I, eight months pregnant, Lorenzo and Camilla, moved to our new home. It was in the heart of Tuscany's most famous wine region, Chianti Classico, half way between Siena and Florence.

CHAPTER FIFTEEN

Friday 5th January 2002, Finn phoned me in a voice tailing off into tears. At 4 o'clock that morning, Nat had tried to commit suicide. The attempt failed and he had been admitted to the psychiatric hospital in Salisbury.

In the middle of the night, he got up, just as he normally did to go to the bathroom. Per usual, he put on his bedroom slippers and dressing gown but instead of going to the bathroom (or perhaps he did that too), went downstairs, unlocked the front door, went out into the night, walked the length of the garden up to the mill pool at the top, and proceeded to wade his way into the icy river, which at that time of year was quite fast flowing and surely not more than 10°C. He then dived forward into the 'pool' itself, five or six feet deep at its deepest. I don't know if he thought he'd drown like this – it wasn't exactly like diving off the North Sea oil rig into the raging sea, but perhaps thought he'd die given his particular medical condition. He could have a heart attack, one last asthma attack, or at the very least, later develop bronchitis or a fatal pneumonia.

But nothing of the sort happened because somehow he managed to make his way back to the house, and there he stood in the hall, dripping wet, freezing, and called out, 'Help!'

I had only just got back to Italy the day before, from sorting out his living situation. We had gone there as a family for Christmas, Lorenzo, I, Camilla - two, and Thomas now nine months old. Nat had been desperate that Christmas holiday - hopeless and helpless - unable to enjoy us, but not allowing us to enjoy ourselves either: he wouldn't let us out of his sight and I remember we couldn't even go and have a glass of beer with some Italian friends staying in the area. He wouldn't allow them in the house either. I'd had a terrible time during the nights because not only was I wakened by our baby Tom, but Nat would have an asthma attack on his journey to the loo, every single night. It was no longer Shelagh who would bear the brunt of this attack, just as I had witnessed in London for our famous family evening out, but I. He would even forewarn me before going to bed making sure that the baby-minder was on, not for baby Tom, but for him. It was for 'just in case I don't make it through the night'. Sure enough, I'd be woken up with his cries for help, he'd tell me he was going to die there and then, and I would coax him back into breathing normally. A Christmas ruined.

"Why does he have to be like this? Why can't he try and enjoy us instead of just getting depressed as soon as we come home? Why can't he be normal?" I moaned to Finn. We'd managed to turn his situation around so that at least we could laugh together. Lorenzo and Finn called him the Black Cloud but translated it into Italian so he became known between us as Nuvola Nera, or just Nuv (Noove) for short.

"I know Cat. He's a bloody pain in the arse! I've never been able to talk to him. He isn't normal," came Finn's reply – a reply loaded with meaning.

There was a great deal of tragedy in Nat's family history. His father who was already sixty years old when Nat was born, died when Nat was only twelve. (That would make my grandfather, were he alive today, a hundred and fifty-four.) Indeed everything about Nat's family was about ancestors - dead people. The stairs in our house were lined with portraits of ancient noble people dressed in ancient clothes. Those paintings with their gilt frames - ladies with white almost translucent skins, austere men rigidly posed - haunted me. Nat's ancestors eyes – Irish ancestors - followed me up and down the stairs. In fact his family tree dates back to 1150 when his ancestor, Dermot King of Leinstar, was born. Finn and I sit at the bottom of this family tree.

Nat was born in Ireland just one year before it gained its independence from the British government. With the signing of the Anglo-Irish Treaty in 1921, after centuries of troubles, at last twenty-six counties in Ireland became together a free state – the now Republic of Ireland. However six largely Protestant counties in the north, chose not to join, and remained separate from the new Irish Free State opting to stay under British rule. It was this separation which brought with it a wave of new and unforeseen troubles – violent troubles - that were indeed to last for decades to follow.

When a man was shot dead outside their front gate, Nat was just two years old. His mother, Caroline (my second name), pregnant with Nat's little brother, David, went into premature labour and died. Baby David lived for six months. After this tragedy, Nat's father was persuaded by his sister, The Ant, to move away from Ireland, as had she. Some years previously she had been held at gunpoint by two young republican soldiers (IRA), who had knocked at her door one evening. Terrified, she left Ireland for good for Somerset in England. I only discovered The Ant's real name when I was inspecting the family tree. Catherine.

But there were other factors from Nat's past, factors that would leave their distinct mark.

Before Shelagh there was the war. He joined up just after he'd started Oxford University. He wanted to join an engineering regiment and become a 'sapper'(the name of engineering privates) but he also wanted to be with his best friend. The friend would never have passed the academic exam to become an engineer, so they both joined the Royal Artillery instead.

On his first day of combat, the friend was killed in action.

While my mother, ten years younger, used to talk about a luxurious childhood in Buenos Aires, Argentina, - 'The Argentine' she called it - with servants and a donkey to carry her golf clubs, Nat was training to become a pilot for the newly founded Army Air Corps – an aviation component of the British army that was not the RAF. He flew planes in enemy territory.

They didn't use proper ear defenders then, so that was why he was so deaf - the engine from the plane being so loud – deafening, literally.

He flew an Auster, a very light two-seated unarmed plane, flying not more than six hundred feet above ground in occupied territory, so low that it couldn't be detected by German radar. His role was to report information by taking photographs. These photographs were quickly and effectively interpreted, so the bombers would know precisely where enemy positions were. In fact air photographs were recognised as essential for controlled bombing. I always liked that my father didn't do any of the bombing himself, that he was involved in protecting, at least to the best of his ability, civilians. What control of one's fear such missions would require. In the end, he was decorated with the DFC – Distinguished Flying Cross – the second highest decoration for bravery.

"Your father is not a brave man." Shelagh said. "What he faced was amazing. But he still did it. Now that's courage."

I have his medal and a signed letter from King George VI, apologising for not being able to present his medal in person. I also found a description of his 'Action for which Commended': '....He has displayed qualities of leadership of a most marked nature....Captain Murray has carried out numerous sorties and has achieved most marked success in locating hostile tanks and infantry and has run many necessary risks from enemy aircraft and fire. His qualities of leadership and gallantry have also been tempered with sound common sense as not one aircraft under his command has been lost through unnecessary risk or avoidable accident.' 4 Nov 1944.

Even more harrowing, he helped liberate the concentration camp Bergen Belsen. I only found this out when 'Schindler's List' came out. I saw the movie and was horrified. We couldn't believe that these things happened in those concentration camps. I asked my father whether he would go to see it.

"No" he said. I can still hear the tone of this 'no' – clipped, definitive, sharp and sure. He'd seen some of the 'making of the movie' on the television. That was enough. He didn't need or want to see the whole film; it was an insult to those who had been in the camps. It infuriated him to see how weak the film was next to the reality.

" You have no idea what it was like" he said in a very controlled voice. " It was nothing like that. Nobody looked like that. Those actors look almost rosy. It was something you people can't possibly imagine." He said no more than that but my mother told me that he had been called to duty that day because the officer who should have gone was away or sick. He wasn't supposed to have gone. I wanted to hear more. Except for this time, he never would talk about it.

But now he was old and tired. And depressed. He couldn't go on living on his own with no one in the house. Of course Finn and I knew we had to do something about it. It was time to return to Tuscany but I needed to stay on a little longer to find a live in carer. So Lorenzo drove back and I stayed on with the children. A nice Irish lady arrived. Her very first night, both mine and Finn's first night back to our respective homes, she was met by her patient, dripping wet in the hall at 4 in the morning calling 'Help.'

I don't think he truly wanted to die, but there's no doubt he wanted us all to come running. It worked of course. His timing was appalling. He knew I was already exhausted by trying to manage our new venture in Tuscany as well as two very small children. Tom had nearly died at nine weeks with encephalitis and I'd been traumatized by the event.

The next day I got a flight straight back and went to visit him with Finn, in the psychiatric institute. We found a wretched-looking shrivelled old man, sitting alone in a shabby foam-cushioned, plastic-covered arm chair. This man was my father. As he looked up his eyes were pools of anxiety and he held them open wide, so wide that he looked like a frightened animal, confused and understanding nothing of his surroundings. His whole obsession with his bowel movements had taken over his mind. He kept saying, "Watch out, don't walk there!! There's shit all over the floor!" All he could see was excrement.

I remember the sweet nurse trying to explain his state and I saw that in some way she was trying to soften the blow of what she imagined must be hurt for us. But there was no pain. I recall thinking as she spoke that she had no idea of the fact that we weren't hurting at all, that she didn't need to protect us. I wanted to tell her how he'd been, how much pain he'd caused, but I felt ashamed and just sat there nodding.

He was kept in the psychiatric hospital and never again spent a single night at Lower Mill. By April there was a space in a very nice nursing home in Salisbury and it was great relief to move him there. Now, we didn't have to worry any more about 'what to do with Nat' or to feel guilty about him. He never again had one asthma attack, never caught even as much as a cold, let alone his usual bronchitis; in fact his physical health was good all things considered. As for his mental suffering, all it took was some *diazepam* to free him of his anxiety, and in turn (perhaps there was other medication as well), he was freed of the depression. His torture was gone and so was ours.

CHAPTER SIXTEEN

"I think I need to go to the hospital." I said to Lorenzo. My voice was calm and normal. "It's for real now."

I got the words out just in time as I leant against the thick stone wall for support. Support that I needed while the onslaught of yet another fierce contraction took a hold of my body. They always tell you to *breath* through the contraction - 'just inhale through your nose and exhale through your mouth' - said in that matter of fact tone, like being asked to just roll up your sleeve or something.

The thing was I'd already been to hospital in the middle of that night, only to find that everything had come to a grinding halt. As much as I'd willed the contractions to pick up, they just fizzled out and I'd had to come home again in the morning, just as pregnant on the journey back from the hospital as I had been on the journey there. It's a very frustrating state to be in, not to mention how stupid you feel. Thomas had done the same trick on me two years before and it had been another five days before he decided it was time to make an entrance into the world.

Therefore, when the contractions started coming on again early that same evening, I wasn't expecting it to be the real thing at all, so I hung on this time.

But now, only half an hour later, there was a force behind each contraction that made me wonder how I could ever have been so easily mistaken before – this was for real now. On and on they came, painfully, relentlessly. Our little baby was decided and her birth was immanent for that same day.

So at 6.30pm, the evening of 13th November 2002, I got in the car for the second time that day to go to hospital. We got there just in time. I remember every curve along the road of that forty-five minute journey. I remember Lorenzo anxiously accelerating as much as he could – our roads are notoriously windy here in Tuscany - I remember the relief we both felt when the hospital came into view and how I waddled along the corridor, resting against the wall there too, every time I was gripped with pain. Finally I made it to the maternity ward and forty minutes later, lying in warm water in one of those marvellous birthing baths, I was holding our little Anna with a teary eyed Lorenzo looking on.

Another being all unto her own. I had created yet another little person, a new person. First one, then two and now three, and each time I felt the magic. And here it had happened all over again.

We tucked her up and brought her home thirty-six hours later and she became a part of our tight knit family as if she'd always been there.

Six months later, on 2nd June 2003 our little nephew Giovanni, Lorenzo's sister, Monica's son, aged seven, died. It is too hard, too sad, too heart wrenching and too personal for me to be able to tell Monica's story here. Besides, it's hers and not mine.

We all just reeled, empty of words.

The day after this, literally, my doctor called me, to inform me that on receiving my biopsy results, I had pre-cancer of the cervix. I should be operated on immediately, it would be better to get this out of the way quickly, he said. Then Finn called, two days later, I thought to ask about Giovanni. But his tone was all wrong. He told me to sit down.

I sat. I wondered what Nat could have possibly done now. Really, his timing was just the worst. I think he did it on purpose. Maximum attention.

"No no, it's not Dad," Finn said. "I have to tell you that I have cancer."

"You have *what?*" It was too unbelievable to be true. Now of all times. No, it wasn't possible.

"You know that ulcer that I've had on my gum – the one that didn't seem to clear up?"

"Umm, yes, now I remember."

"Well they did a biopsy on it and it's come out positive. It's cancer."

I felt my heart go into panic mode. I gabbled out a mess of words, words to convince myself more than anything, that he would be alright.

The thing was, Finn wasn't living in England any more but temporarily in Italy. Perhaps in part because of me but also because he'd been given an opportunity to give London a break for a year. His old best friend from school had set up a language school in the city of Trento, and, doing quite well now, needed some assistance with the accounting which was all under British legislation. What better person to come and deal with it, than his old friend Finn?

Finn had seemed happy up there – happier than he had ever been in London - and came every two or three weeks to visit us. It was nice being nearer together now. He'd joined a choir. His Italian got good. He'd got away from Nat.

And here he was now, telling me he had cancer. He didn't have Italian health care and even if he did, I wasn't in a position to look after him. There was no one there who could take him to and from hospital, cook him a meal, or give him a simple hug. I ached inside at the thought of his predicament.

"I'm going to go back to England. I can stay with Alan and Rosemary," and his words gave me a relative sense of relief. These were friends of his from our village back home. A refuge for Finn when Nat used to get too much for him. Kind loving people.

So this is what he did. He left Trento and drove himself all the 1500km by himself.

All the while the tumour grew bigger. Just before he left, he told me, it was the size of a golf ball and you could see it bulging from his cheek.

I could now feel the severity of the situation through the airwaves. He was home and seeing surgeons. Surgeons from the Plastic, Oral and Maxillo-facial department. He and Rosemary called it Max-fax. They were good at joking. Sometimes it's the only way to get through these things. Drastic measures would be needed, Rosemary told me. Immediately.

"What do drastic measures entail?" My heart beat fast as I clutched the telephone.

"Well, they're going to take out his lower jaw bone from the joint, right round to the other side of his face and nearly reaching the joint the other side."

"What? Take it all out? The whole bone? But, but, I mean," I couldn't finish my sentence.

" They are going to replace it with the fibula from his leg. They say we have an extra bone which apparently we can do very well without. Then they're going to shape it to follow the contour and curve of the jaw." Rosemary sounded so confident. I felt numb.

"That's incredible," was all I could manage and I felt the weakness of my expression beside the magnitude of the reality.

"I know. I couldn't believe it myself but he's going to ok Catriona. They're just amazing. They're extremely positive, all of the surgeons. Then they explained that they will use skin from another part of his body to create the gum, called a 'flap'. They have two teams of eight surgeons. They think it should be about fourteen hours altogether."

It was only after I put the phone down that I registered the tenseness in my body. I just sat there staring at the floor, numb.

Salisbury hospital was and is a top specialist centre for plastic surgery in the South of England. He was in the best place. This was because Salisbury Plain is filled with military bases and has been for decades, hence why we lived there. After the D-Day landings in World War Two, a special unit for burns was built, a state-of the-art for its time. The hospital has became the centre for specialist services in particular, burns and plastic surgery and spinal injuries, ever since.

They operated on him on 26th June. I too had my own small operation, not the same day but nearly. I came out of hospital, and three days later I was given the all clear – no more pre-cancer cells. My operation had taken twenty minutes, his twenty hours. He was in intensive care. He was conscious but still on a respirator. His face had been opened up via his neck which was now stapled back together. His leg had a cast on it. His lymph nodes in his neck had been removed as they too were infected. His main nerve in his cheek had been unavoidably severed during surgery so he would not be able to hold up the muscle on that side of his face, making it look deformed or as if he'd had a vey heavy stroke all drooping down. His 'flap' was huge making his lower lip bulge out. He would be on crutches for a while.

All in all the doctors were very pleased with how it had gone.

At the same time, we were coping with the intricacies of our Tuscan venture; life still had to go on. There was always so much to do. Dealing with one child or baby, nursing in the middle of the night, preparing baby food, and so on, would have been plenty, but the apartments and guests needed taking care of, just as the vineyard and winery too.

On Saturdays there was the task of cleaning all nine apartments, and in the first year, there was a mountain of sheets and towels to launder. Leanne, one of our helpers, used to come in the mornings. She was fabulous and would do anything. Sometimes she'd look after the children while I would go back and forth between laundry room and washing lines. There was certainly no shortage of lines, or sunshine for that matter, but I could have done with triple length arms. I would get myself in quite a twist with sheets that seemed to have a secret pact with the wind. Folding them too became a test of both patience and arm muscle stamina. Then Leanne and I between us would iron the whole lot. It would take us all week from one Saturday to the next. I don't why it took us two years to realize that the simple solution was to take them to the laundry service in the village.

2003 was a drought summer in Italy. By now we'd mastered the art of change-over day, made improvements to the apartments, had a pool built, which brought in more bookings, so that in full summer, our apartments were bulging – twenty-eight guests in total. Our farm, almost a community, was alive and buzzing with people from all over the world.

The pool required yet more work. Pools are notoriously high maintenance. Lorenzo would religiously clean it every morning before guests were up to fill it. Usually this would involve changing the filters, checking the chlorine levels, and cleaning the floor of the pool with one of those special vacuum machines with lots of floating plastic tube. Sometimes he would have to fish out a dead mouse floating on the surface – one who'd bent down for a drink and fallen in and drowned. One morning, he saw yet another one, floating there near the border, but it was the movement of this mouse that caught his eye. It was still alive – just – desperately fighting for life. So Lorenzo rescued the little creature with the fly net, and gently placed it down on the tiles. I can almost hear the little mouse thanking Lorenzo, like Stuart Little. "Thank you thank you kind man! What can I do for you in return?" Lorenzo carried on with his vacuuming, and forgetting Stuart Little was there, took a step back, and, squelch. What a pity.

That year of 2003 was stiflingly hot and temperatures soared to 40°C. In Florence, it was higher. Being outside was unbearable. We had to close all the doors, windows and shutters at about 10am so as to keep the cooler air inside and not let any of the day's heat in. With such thick stone walls, this method was effective. But still with three small children, the heat zapped one's energy. With twenty-eight guests in our apartments to keep happy, I felt fatigued and frustrated. I just had to get back to see my brother after his marathon operation.

I left a week later in the middle of July, taking six month old Anna with me. Alan Willis came to meet us at the airport. It was nice to be met. He told me a little of Finn's condition and how he looked. I was dreading the moment. I should have been used to it.

Finn came forward walking with the use of two crutches. He was looking straight at me, never taking his eyes away. I saw sadness in them. That's what I saw first. It was sadness for me, not him, that I had to behold him like this. Then behind the sadness was defiance. There was still boldness in his hobble. A smile spread out from the good half of his misshapen swollen mouth, while the bad half drooped grotesquely down to one side. He rested his crutches down against the hall table. I rushed to hug him.

He was going to live.

CHAPTER SEVENTEEEN

Once back home in Tuscany, to a certain extent, I was distracted – my days were so full and I wasn't physically with Finn - but then at the same time, the worry had taken residence inside of me and his predicament was always there, a constant presence like a cloud hovering above my head, with anything that I did.

Sometimes you can be listening to another person – or rather pretend to be listening - looking right at them, even nodding in agreement, but in reality you are not registering a single word of what they are saying. It was like this for me with everything that I was doing. I was on autopilot. I could be explaining to a guest about how to get to the Uffizzi Gallery in Florence - animated and smiling - or be spoon feeding little Anna or answering the telephone, but all the time, my mind was elsewhere. I was back in England. I was in the hospital. I was in the operating theatre. I was back at Rosemary's house. In fact I can't remember that summer as far as our farm and family life went at all – what we did or who was here – I can only remember the heat. The heat and Finn.

I spoke to Finn's leading consultant. I had managed to fix a time to call, and used the telephone down in our reception where I knew the children wouldn't disturb me. I needed space. Dr. Sandy was positive. It would be just a question of time before Finn would be fully recovered and able to re-think what he wanted to do with his life. As for his face, Dr. Sandy told me, they could later put in 'slings' on the inside of his cheek which would hold up the muscle and his face would look almost perfect. Then they could put in dental implants.

I then asked the fatal question.

"But has his cancer gone? I mean is there any risk of it coming back?"

I knew the answer before the question had left my mouth.

"We have no means of knowing but of course we would like to believe so. We will always hope that Finn will make a full and permanent recovery."

I had wished for the impossible. How could a doctor say anything different? *'No it will never come back'* - the one and only acceptable answer. But this could never be said and it was the unmentionable thought - to lose Finn – which would not be bearable.

Finn's goal for the year was to come to Italy for Anna's christening.

Now it was November and his trip was planned. Rosemary was phoning me often. She was anxious about him. He'd started complaining of back pain and she worried that the trip would take a lot out of him but he was adamant that he wanted to come and furthermore that he would drive himself to Gatwick airport.

I wasn't really sure what to expect: I had a sense of foreboding on one hand but on the other I was buoyed by Finn's determination and courage. In the middle of the month, Lorenzo went to pick him up from the airport at Pisa.

He stayed a week. But it was a week of pain – pain so bad he couldn't sleep at night.

Now I was even more frightened.

He had scans to find the source of the pain on his return home. I waited for his phone call to tell me the results. I knew what to expect. I'd seen the change – the change in his nature. "Finn, what's twenty per cent of fifty-five thousand euro?" I didn't need to know but I did need to recognize my brother I asked while he'd stayed for Anna's christening.

"Um," he had paused. He had looked vague. The usual animation and brightness, gone. He had tried to crunch the numbers through his head. He failed. He hadn't seemed to care. Where were his enthusiasm, his mental vigour and eventual triumph?

Where was Finn?

Now I clutched the telephone with dread. His shaky voice told me that he had six tumours in his spine, another around his neck area, and two in his arm. He had full-blown bone cancer. The most painful cancer of all.

What did I say to him? What words did I find to reply? What comfort did I give him? I was falling. Falling into a black hole. I knew there were no more corners to turn. There were no more answers. There could be no salvation now.

The unmentionable was now the reality.

I lose track here of which week or which day was which - things were moving so fast - but I remember that it became difficult for Rosemary to look after him at home, and he was admitted to Salisbury Palliative care unit where they could keep his pain under control and where they knew so well how to look after him. I knew this place as Shelagh had spent some time in there. I knew what it meant too.

A phone call from Alan Willis now. Finn had a large deep vein thrombosis in his leg. Why did I hear Alan trying to be sensitive, tactful? Why was he talking to me in this voice? My heart raced. "Well, you see Cat, it's not so much a question of *if* parts of it will break off and reach his heart, but *when.* When that happens, it will cause a heart attack. They can't say when, but it *will* happen you see." I breathed. "And as you are his next of kin, you need to give your word on whether he should be resuscitated or not, when this happens. If they did manage to resuscitate, they don't know how much of his brain might be damaged – what state he would be in after – and the cancer is killing him so quickly now. It would just be more suffering for him, to keep him alive like this."

I got the picture. I got it quickly. I tired to grab at the possibility of it "being worth resuscitation", but time was running out - like watching a sand timer – his time, and a helpless sense of panic gripped me.

"Let him go."

I put the phone down and felt like I'd signed his death warrant. I looked at Lorenzo who was sitting on the sofa. The children were in bed. Lorenzo held me and cried. He really cried. We held onto one another tight.

Then the most unusual thing occurred. Camilla, six, who had been fast asleep and who would rarely wake, was all of a sudden standing in the doorway. She saw us both in this state. It was terrible. I felt awful, awful. I took her back to her bed and cuddled her and reassured her that we weren't hurting ourselves at all; it was Finn. I told her the truth.

As soon as possible, we packed up the car and took all three children with us back to England. I'd had to tell myself that that if he died while I was in the middle of France somewhere, then that was just the way it was meant to be.

But he didn't die. They always wait for you. Of that I'm now quite certain. "Hello Cat," he said as I walked in. He was sitting up supported by many pillows. The impact of the first meeting is always the hardest. Then you get used to it, and you cope. I saw how old his face looked, there were wrinkles on his cheeks, so out of place for a face that had been perennially young and plump.

We talked. I don't know what about. I don't remember any painful silences.

There was something very special about the Palliative Care Unit. You felt the kindness as soon as you entered. There was nothing sordid or horrific. Not even pitiful. An uncomplicated 'hello Catriona' and a smile, in the corridor as you passed a nurse you'd just met the day before. A carpeted and quite homely corridor. Nothing clinical. You were never told to 'just go and take a seat in the waiting room'. There was no waiting room. You might be asked, 'would you like a cup of tea?' and then to go and help yourself in the kitchen. Or be told where the playroom for children is, and therein find an assortment of toys games and books. You felt your loved one was safe too – they took the weight of responsibility off your shoulder with their efficient know-how ways. Their patients solely ones who had no chances left, where time – every minute, every second – became so precious, yet they always had time for you.

These nurses were the kind of people you'd like to pack up in your suitcase and take home with you. They were people who *chose* to work here, chose to work with people whose only task was to die. One told me that the reason she loved her work was because she saw more love here, than in any other place. I chewed on the thought. What about babies being born? What about all the people who come joyously rushing to maternity wards? What about weddings and all the love flowing there too? But on reflection, perhaps there's more love at a funeral than a wedding.

Then there was still Nat to be considered. He was losing his son and it was too much for me to give him comfort and support too. He got a taxi to the hospital to visit him, but the visits were strained and difficult for both of them with neither knowing what to say. It was better if I was there too.

I did have a proper talk with a doctor just once. I couldn't hold the tears in this time though. I just couldn't get one single word out. I sat there at the side of her desk and she handed me tissues and watched me sob. I couldn't stop. I wanted to know how much time he had. Time. But how could they know? A week? A month? Perhaps he might go even tonight. 'A few weeks' was all she could say. Was that all that was left for him? I had my entire life still in front of me, so much still to do, and Finn who was not even forty, had no future any more at all.

On Christmas Eve before we went to the cathedral, as I was leaving, Finn said he'd like to accompany me along the corridor to the door. I was pleased because the visit had been very stilted, cold and formal because my father had come too. I didn't want to leave on that note. I'd brought Nat myself but had told him that a taxi could take him back as I needed to rush off to the cathedral. I couldn't really bear being around him if truth were told. As we walked slowly along, Finn put his hand through my arm. He said, "I have to tell you something Cat. I'm going to die."

"I know." I replied and we both looked ahead.

We rounded the corner of the corridor. At the end was the door to the outside. We stopped half way along. I looked at him straight in his eyes holding them with mine, and without even a glance to the ground, I said, "Are you scared of dying?"

"No" he said. "I'm not frightened. Are *you* scared of me dying?"

"No, not really. Mum's already there. She'll be waiting for you."

"Yes, I know."

"I'm just going to miss you really badly when you're not here any more." I began to cry. "I'm going to really miss you. You're the only brother I've ever had and will ever have." I was sobbing.

His eyes filled with tears and he held me as I wept in his arms.

We looked at each other. We just carried on standing there neither wanting the moment to end. But it had to end.

"Well, I'd better be off. I'm going to the carol service."

"Yes. You go. Bye."

"Love you. Bye Finn."

"Love you too."

I turned and walked towards the exit. He turned and walked back towards his room. Just before I opened the door, I took one last look over my shoulder to wave at him. But he was intent on the task of moving forward and I saw him in profile as he disappeared around the corner. He never turned to look back.

I inhaled the cold night air in the car park outside and felt a sense of joy - it was such a *relief*. We had shared the Truth and I discovered that there is nothing in this world so pure. There was nothing to be afraid of any more, no more words to be said, no words held back in fear. It was the joy of Love.

He died the next day. I held his hand as I watched his breathing, his pulse. I saw his last breath.

When I come to the end of the road,
And the sun has set for me,
I want no tears in a gloom filled room,
Why cry for a soul set free?

Miss me a little, but not too much
And not with your head bowed low,
Remember the love that we once shared,
Miss me, but let me go.

For this is a journey we all must take
And each must go alone;
It is all part of God's perfect plan
A step on the road to home.

When you are lonely and sick of heart
Go to the friends that we know
And bury your sorrows in doing good.
Miss me, but let me go.   (Christina Rossetti)

I stood in front of one hundred and sixty people and read this. I managed, only just, to read it in a steady voice. I came back to sit down next to my father, and as I squeezed his hand, I felt him squeeze mine back.

I had been here in the same church six and a half years previously for my mother and I saw the same love and sympathy worn on the faces of the people looking at me again. Now for my brother.

I *was* "lonely and sick of heart." My childhood family had disappeared. I was floating in grief, cut off from my past. There was no one left. If the souls of Finn and Shelagh had been "set free", I was left behind. The church was so full that people were spilling out of the door. All people who had loved him or who had been touched by him in some way were there, even Dr. Sandy who had dedicated so much of his time to trying to save Finn, was there. I didn't know him but knew it was testament to

Finn. That was how it was. I also regret that Lorenzo too couldn't quite find it in himself to bear the pain, and be there to support and share it with me. He didn't come.

I was bereft. I was on roller coaster of grief. Nothing could take away the pain. This was how 2004 began. I would therefore never have been able to imagine possible, the extraordinary events that followed. Events that didn't so much change the course of my life, but my vision of it.

PART TWO

CHAPTER EIGHTEEN

I was choking, drowning; tears pricked easily. I missed Finn so much, a coma seemed a pleasant option. There I could sleep – hide. Sleep was elusive. I was in a permanent state of exhaustion – that exhaustion which comes from sleep deprivation. It became my daily way of being. Night after night I would go to bed in dread of being awake hour after hour. No one could help me - Lorenzo didn't know how – and having children did not lift me – *everything* was a burden. A friend suggested I go to see someone – a therapist – who could teach me how to relax and sleep better.

I don't think you realize when you have reached a turning point in your life. At any rate, not while you are in the middle of doing the turning as it were. But it was here that everything was about to change: I had reached my crossroads.

I was brought to the doorstep of a seventy-year-old therapist in the middle of Florence. Her name was Dott.ssa Anna Pesci.

I didn't really know – or care - what therapy was. I knew people went to *'talk'* – talk about their problems – but as far as I was concerned, I didn't have any – I just had this terrible pain and there was nothing that could be done to take it away. Little did I know that I would start on a journey - an unravelling of self and of history – which would change everything.

My therapist, in her seventies, with grey Einstein-hair, dressed always with an exotic twist, something unexpected, never wavered from her dignified yet compassionate disposition. I would go to see her for a few hours a week and within the safely and comfort of her four walls, she would absorb me into her care and understanding. Later and over the years, she would guide me through my maze of confusion, by giving me the tools to find my own clarity. She did not teach me new thoughts, but how to think them.

I have learned through her that if we can dismantle the seemingly inflexible network of our life long held assumptions, mostly unconscious ones, and then have the strength to reconstruct them from scratch, we can change the story that dominates our life. We change ourselves. At long last I understand that we see things in the world, not as *they* are, but as *we* are.

As I talked, or rather cried, my way through my mother's death, my brother's all too recent death, unloading the immense pain I was carrying inside, I expressed my desperation over not being able to hold myself up, let alone my children or husband who so needed me, and feeling I was failing them and failing myself.

Then almost by chance, I added - a sort of in brackets 'by the by' - that I was adopted. Being so used to people's reaction to this – one of curiosity - I was surprised by the heightened way she was alerted. There was something very new to me in her response, certainly as if this fact carried much more weight than anything else that I had told her so far, but also like every part of me was hinging on it. When I'd finished, she asked if my birth mother (still unknown to me then) had ever come looking for me.

"No." I said.

"*Eri abandonata dalla tua prima madre che ti ha avuto, secondo dai tuoi genitori che ti hanno mandato via cosi giovane, e tre, dalla madre che hai avuto perché è morta. Adesso dal tuo fratello – morto anche lui. Quante volte una persona può essere buttata via?*" ["You were abandoned first by the mother who had you," she counted one with her thumb, "then by your parents who sent you away so young," two on her next finger, "three because the mother who you did have, died, and now by your brother." She went on, "How many times can a person be thrown away?"]

Thrown away? What misplaced sympathy. My pain was not about ever having been discarded as she put it. I defended my parents and their choices defiantly. As for being *abandoned* by my birth mother – what a strong word - I felt indignant.

I underwent a test – an analysis through pictures, questions and answers, drawings – but felt a little silly, and wondered where it could all be going. She read out the 'results' in the next session, describing my current state of being.

"You've been hiding behind a mask, a mask that you have created. You've been mystifying yourself – in denial."

I didn't get it at all.

Then when she told me that my adoptive mother could never replace my birth mother, or rather, *my birth mother's love*, all I could do was stare at her, mute. What on earth was she talking about? She was saying that the Nature was more important than the Nurture? Was that it? Shelagh was a wonderful mother! Nurture was everything. Her love was supreme. Of course I could be loved and nurtured by her instead. And mask? How could she suggest I was disguising myself?

"Well, no, it's not that. I have no doubt your adoptive mother was a good mother. I have no doubt that she loved you. I'm not saying she didn't," she explained, " but your real mother's love is still missing."

"No it's not! My birth mother loved me surely? She had me for goodness sake! I'm sure she still loves me." I was indignant now. Missing maternal love did not sit comfortably with me. Shelagh had filled the space more than adequately. "I bet my birth mother never stopped thinking about me and anyway, she didn't leave me! She gave me up."

"Caterina," as she called me, "It's the same thing. Whatever reason she had, that's not love. Or rather, it's not love as far as her baby is concerned. You have to understand that love is a behaviour, not words. How can a baby – and later a child or grown woman as you are now – know her mother's love if the mother is simply not there, never been there? Gone. Left. That behaviour translates as anything *but* love. It's *not* an act of kindness. It's *not* generous, or courageous, or good – she

103

abandoned you! Do you understand? Your mother abandoned you. So she *didn't* love you. How can abandonment be love? Shelagh can love you for all you want, but it can never make your birth mother's love, how can I explain," she paused, "*be.* Come into existence. Your birth mother's love does not exist. *That* is what makes you so insecure. Your missing maternal love. Do you understand?"

Sort of. Well not really.

"So you pretend instead," she went on. "You've been pretending all your life. That's the denial. Pretending to be another one's daughter – pretend that you *have* your real maternal love when it's actually still missing. Pretending that she didn't really abandon you. Then you crawl inside the skin of your adoptive mother's baby – the one that was never conceived, never existed - instead of living inside your own. You try to make yourself become her in order to be loved. Perhaps your brother never did this - liken himself - pretending to be someone else. You've convinced yourself into being born from your adoptive mother, as if you *are* her genes, her reflection, when the reality is that you are not. You come from another. You can't be something you're not. You can't fit a square peg into a round hole."

It's a weird thing to be able to count only on one hand, the number of people who can say that they knew me as a child. But that's the way it is. We never had much of a greater family – no grandparents (apart from Dorothy with dementia), no aunts or uncles so no first cousins, and only distant cousins who we never really knew. Tania Robertson though, now *she* knew me as a child. Tania Robertson was the other girl who had been standing against the big front door of my first boarding school, the girl who had just stared at me. I wouldn't know her today were it not for the fact that we both chose the same university in London to do a teaching training degree course and we re-met and became friends. At university I learned she too was adopted.

My search for my birth mother began when Tania came to stay.

I have to say that we adoptees feel like a breed. We are somehow connected by an invisible thread – an unspoken kindred spirit. So it wasn't really the vocation of teaching that drew us together as friends, but this.

After Finn had died, Tania, now a mother too, came to Tuscany to stay with us. Here I was astonished to learn that she had searched for and found her birth mother. I listened to her story in amazement. How could a mother not want to know her own daughter? Let alone not even admit she had even had her.

Suddenly my own curiosity about my birth mother resurfaced. We talked.

"It could be that my birth mother is in Canada – I know she came back to have me in England, but maybe she went back to Canada after. Or maybe she stayed in England."

"Yes but her birth records would be in England and maybe even marriage. We can find out."

"How?" I hadn't a clue. Tania told me that the first thing I needed was a name. My name.

"Your *birth* name, Cat! You were called something different when you were born."

"Oh, yes of course. Jane. My name was Jane."

"Yes but you need to know your surname. You'll be registered in the birth section at the GRO under your surname. Then we can find your birth certificate and find out your mother's name and where she lived. You do have a real birth certificate too like every one else you know – you can only be born once and you were born by your birth mother, right?"

My name. My surname. Birth certificate. Where my birth mother lived? It felt weird just thinking about the possibility of her existence, let alone finding her.

Yes I had always known that my name had been Jane, and that my birth mother had been nineteen, but I hadn't thought about the surname. However, when Finn and I sold our family home and Nat was in a nursing home, when Finn was going through piles and piles of papers in Nat's little studio, he came across two pieces of paper, one with my original name, and one with his own. At the time he phoned me to tell me.

"Cat do you want to know what your name was?"

"Well tell me then. I'm Jane something aren't I?" I replied.

"Yes, you were Jane Richardson." It meant nothing to me. Only a name. It didn't identify me – I had my own identity already.

"What were you?"

"Michael Fanshawe." Finn told me.

"Fanshawe? What kind of a surname is that?" and we laughed together.

So I was able to tell Tania that my surname was Richardson. As we talked, she grew more and more enthusiastic and said that she could go to the GRO for me and pickup a copy of her friend Jane Richardson's birth certificate for her. Again I felt strange, like something was dawning – an awakening. That I was that Jane Richardson - Jane Richardson was me - and yet I couldn't shake the nonsensical image that she was somebody else - looking at her birth certificate was trespassing. It was private property. Not mine.

Some weeks later, Lorenzo came into the house waving a brown manila envelope.

"Who's Jane Richardson?"

"That's me!" Looking at this now all-powerful manila envelope, I grabbed it and eagerly ripped open the seal. Here inside was both my name and my birth mother's name. Loud and clear. Name and Surname of Mother: Hope Jennifer Richardson of Scribbins of Worplesdon.

 Name and Surname of Father: "undisclosed".

'Is that *it*?' I thought. This is all I get? What *had* I been expecting?

Scribbins? What a strange name for a 'mother and baby home'. Worpleston? I'd never heard of Worpleston. So I looked it up on the map. Near Guildford. My birthplace.

Hope? Hope. I rolled the name around my head. 'Her name was Hope,' I said to myself, not thinking to put that thought in the present tense.

What didn't make sense, was that a 'Mother and Baby Home' should be called Scribbins. Wouldn't it have a more formal name? Like what? 'The Caring Trust', 'The Family Clinic'. I knew that the vast majority of pregnant young women who were sent to have their babies in secret went to mother and baby homes. My mother must have done the same. But Scribbins? What kind of name was that?

Tania and I talked again. It had been easy to find me.

"You first go to the 'birth' section. Then you find the year. Then you find the right quarter - July is the third one of 1965. Then you go through that ledger chronologically and then for the date, it will be in alphabetical order. There was only one Jane Richardson born on 18th July 1965. It had to be you!" she said.

Then you make a note of the entry number, go to the reception and apply for a certified copy of that entry. This is what I had in my hand now.

"Ok, well if you want I can go back and start looking up H.J. Richardson." She offered. It was like detective work.

"Where though?"

"Well, if we know her age when you were born, what did you say, nineteen?"

"Yes, as far as I know, nineteen."

"Then I'll look for her birth certificate between 1945 and 1946. That'll give us lots of information on where she is from, the names of her parents. Then her marriage certificate between, let's say 1965 and 1970. Then if I can find that, we'll know what her name is now, and be able to find her. Hopefully."

Easy.

A couple of weeks later Tania e-mailed me.

*'Hi Cat, I have taken the journey a little further today…
I have hopefully found your mum's birth cert – her mother's maiden name was Auckland! She was born June-Sept 1946 in Bournemouth. I then spent about an hour searching the years around that date for another Richardson/Auckland baby combination and between 1943-49 I didn't see one. I think I scanned 7000 names!! What this means is that in that time frame, there doesn't seem to be a sibling. I have also looked for marriages from Sept 1965 to end 1970. Four Hope Richardsons got married then… but only 2 with Hope J. Richardson. I have ordered both.*

Hope J. Richardson married Thomas A. Creamer (bad surname!) Summer 1968 in Brent; Hope J. Richardson married Michael J. Cunningham in Spring 1970 in Stoke on Trent. Fingers crossed one of these turns out to be yours. Be prepared we might be barking up the wrong tree. Sorry if I'm being factual – I'm dead beat but still really excited for you!'

The marriage certificates of both Hope J Richardson's arrived but they weren't her. Neither middle name turned out to be Jennifer.

Dead end.

CHAPTER NINETEEN

June 2004 and Finn hadn't even been gone six months. I was on my way up to England having decided to take up the Willis's offer to bring the children and come and stay a while. I didn't really care where I was or what I did. Why not? I decided to stay a whole month and Lorenzo would look after the farm.

Shortly after my arrival, I received an e-mail from a Mrs Susan Warnock. I had taken her on as an accredited researcher who I found through NORCAP, an organization supporting adults in the adoption triangle. I thought she might find something Tania had missed. But Hope Jennifer Richardson was nowhere to be found. There was simply record of her, as if she didn't exist.

However she did one thing Tania had not. She went through electoral roles of 1965 of the district of Guildford trying to find a name for the address Scribbins of Worpleston. She was then able to tell me that a couple had been living there in 1965 and their name was Akehurst. She was also able to tell me that he – Mr Peter Akehurst - had died and that she, Mrs Eileen Akehurst, elderly now, had moved to Yorkshire. She advised me to try and get in touch with Mrs Akehurst or to try and reach my own records in the archives of the borough council where I was born, as an alternative plan of action. Perhaps there might be some information about the identity of the father.

As I digested this information, I pictured the old lady in Yorkshire. She must have had something to do with the Mother and Baby Home and maybe she had even set eyes on

Hope. But how could she possibly remember? I felt this whole thing was futile.

"Oh well, who cares, this was obviously 'not meant to be,'" I told Rosemary. "This old lady would hardly have a record of the girls' whereabouts today."

I gave up.

One Wednesday evening while still there at the Willis's, I came back from a day out with all three children (Anna not yet two years old, Tom four and Camilla six), to be met with two bright excited faces who 'had something to tell me'.

"We've got some exciting news," said Rosemary. I didn't even realize she was talking about the search.

"Well, I just couldn't stop thinking about such a small village. I mean it must be the size of our village here, and well, just like here, there must be people still there who were there in 1965."

"Mmm," my ears pricked up.

"And a village would not be a village without its gossip. So I thought if I tried asking at the post office, they'd be able to tell me who was living there back then." She was so bright eyed. She had more to tell me.

"So? Go on," I was getting a little excited now.

"Well I've just been talking for one hour with Sue from the post office of Worpleston!"

"Wow, really?"

"Yes, and guess what?"

"What?"

"Scribbins never was a mother and baby home. It's a private home and the Akehurst's were a family living there in the sixties until the end of the eighties. And guess what? They're *Canadian*! There are three children – well grown up now - called Jennifer," stressing the name 'Jennifer' with a knowing look to me, "Ben and Quentin. Ben and Quentin live in Yorkshire where Eileen, the mother lives, and Jennifer lives in Guernsey!" She had my full attention. "Want more?"

"Yes yes go on. I can't believe this," I replied, more to myself, staring into space as I digested the information.

"She knew all sorts of things. That Quentin had divorced, that the father had died and he had been very deaf. Everybody knew this family!"

"What about Hope though? Did she know who Hope was?"

"Well, she thought she'd heard something about a young girl living with them who used to help with the horses and said that yes, maybe there was some kind of scandal about being pregnant!"

I had an image of a young girl – not connected to me in any way – just a young pregnant girl. I saw her hanging out the washing on a line in a garden, slim but with a bulging tummy, soft brown hair like mine, blowing in the breeze.

"She also said that Peter Akehurst had been a bit of a Jack the Lad. You know, a womanizer. I mean maybe *he* had got her pregnant!" Goodness, I thought. Yes that could be it. I was trying to digest this thought but I couldn't conjure up any image.

Suddenly after just one hour, no forms, no appointments, no ledgers or lists, and without even having gone anywhere - just listening to village gossip - this remarkable news had been uncovered. All the hours and days of Tania's work, Kathy Warnock's work, through the official and correct channels, had been to no avail.

We surmised, discussed, deduced and hypothesized. Maybe there was some ugly story and they wouldn't want to discuss or divulge. Something secret about the father. What should we do next? Alan said he thought we should simply go there ourselves. We should meet Sue at the post office and see if we could glean any more information either from her or anybody else. Perhaps we could even find this house with the odd name.

Two days later, Friday 16th July 2004, with three small children in tow, Alan, Rosemary and I set off. Within an hour and a half, we were at the post office of the village of Worpleston. Ten minutes later, outside the gate to the entrance of 'Scribbins'. The owners were now people called Thorne.

"This can't be it?" I exclaimed.

I was peering over the gate at small wooden bungalow. It was so out of place here in this quintessentially English village. No thatching for a roof, no flint stones or old bricks, just dark horizontal planks of wood. It looked peculiar.

A lady came to the gate. She was accompanied by two or three large barking dogs.

"One moment – I'll just put these beasts away – they make such a racket!" And in her voice there was friendliness, which I hadn't expected. What *had* I been expecting?

As Rosemary and I stood in the middle of the driveway, Alan in the car with the children, I asked the lady, "This might sound rather an odd reason to be knocking on your door, but my name is Catriona. Catriona Murray. I'm adopted and I'm doing some research to find my birth mother. She apparently lived in this house when I was born in 1965. Would you know anything? Her name was Hope Richardson. We were given directions by the lady from the post office who told us about the Akehurst family who lived here. All we know is that the late Peter Akehurst was a Canadian Jack the Lad and that they had three children and have all moved to Yorkshire."

"Oh, well we only came here in 1990. We bought the house from the Akehursts so we met them. Peter died I heard and I wouldn't know about him being a Jack the Lad - he certainly wasn't when we met him - he was very ill with cancer. They were Canadian."

The helpful and sympathetic way Mrs Thorne had, surprised me.

"I'm sorry I'm not able to be more helpful. I think you could try asking the Cunninghams. They would have known the Akehursts." She told us where to find their house.

We drove to the new address. Leaving the car and my companions parked on the road outside, I stood in front of another stranger's door feeling a little more rehearsed, but still not without trepidation.

You see, when you've been taught all your life that the mother who gave birth to you, has chosen not to know you, however disguised and cushioned this information - couldn't keep you - you feel that she, poor woman, has all the rights to her anonymity, more from you than anyone else. It never occurs to you that to find her, to therefore unveil her, is *not* to trespass, but that you are simply following a basic human instinct and human right.

But even if I'd considered that, I still would have felt I was breaking a law, not *the* law, but *her* law. And for this I was going down a road that wasn't mine. Surely anyone who knew anything, would react with suspicion, or with aggression. At the very least, doors would be slammed in my face. There existed a very deep-rooted fear. A fear of not being wanted by her a second time, and *that* feeling was powerful.

So when, having interrupted Mr and Mrs Cunningham's lunch and invaded their private space, as I stood in their kitchen, I a total stranger to them and they to me, of course I was surprised to be met with two people not only ready to listen to my questions, but interested too, and even sympathetic and keen to help in any way.

They too knew all about deaf Mr Peter Akehurst, who could be heard yelling for his dogs across the common. He was famous for that in the village. Eccentric.

"Let me telephone Eleanor. She's been here the longest. Eleanor Hathaway." And off she went into the other room. Would she mind if a nice young woman came around to ask some questions about the Akehursts? Oh, I think it's better if she tells you herself.

Directions in hand like a clue on a treasure hunt, we set off to find the next house. Suddenly it felt as if there was some kind of greater plan in the making: instead of trespassing on prohibited territory, this was a 'meant to be', and the hand of goodness was leading me to my destination.

Now we found ourselves outside a typical English cottage, red bricked with a thatched roof that nearly coming down to ground level. There was a wooden gate with a latch and a path to the front door.

It opened before Rosemary and I even got there. Mrs Hathaway welcomed us in and we sat in her small sitting room. She can't have been more than five feet tall. Although her bright eyes reflected a sharp presence, she moved in a fairly arthritic fashion. She told us she was eighty-four.

"Now, I understand you'd like to know about the Akehursts." I sat opposite her in my white jeans and navy blue jacket.

"Well yes Mrs Hathaway. The thing is this…" I went on.

"Well isn't it *extraordinary*? Quentin and Eileen were here just last week on their way back up to Yorkshire. Eileen had just got back from a trip to Canada and Quentin was picking her up!"

She told us about the Akehursts – they were close friends – about Quentin's divorce and the children and Jennifer had adopted a little girl from China and Ben had two small children and Quentin two girls. A bundle of information but nothing about Hope.

"Would you know anything about Hope? Hope Richardson?" I questioned. Now at last the information I needed would come.

"No. Never heard of her. I came here in 1968", came a clipped answer. A sudden contrast to her interest and sweetness.

In that instant I knew I'd touched on secrets she knew but was forbidden to disclose. I had no words. It was Rosemary who saved the moment. "I was thinking that if she was pregnant and coming here to have the baby in secret, then, who would a young girl go to live with? I mean, surely one would choose family? The Akehursts must have been relatives of hers and surely quite close ones?"

I can remember how Mrs Hathaway's head turned towards me as if in slow motion. I'll never forget the change in her expression, the way her eyes lit up. She looked straight at me.

"Oh, yes, *now* maybe I remember something!" and her voice tailed off into her own silent deductions. "Wait a moment, I could telephone a friend who was here before me who knows the Akehursts ever so well. Jane Henderson." I listened again to a phone conversation in another room as yet another clue in our hunt had been reached.

"Yes, well I'll call her and you can speak to her yourself." I was summoned to the other room.

I held the telephone like holding a lifeline. My lifeline. What would this Jane have to say? What did she know? "I remember Hope." She said in a simple and matter of fact way. No hesitation. "She was pregnant I think. Wasn't there some story of an illegitimate baby?"

This was the first time in the thirty-nine years of my life that Hope, even if still in the past, became a real flesh and blood person. Someone knew her, or had known her. This person with whom I was talking on the telephone, had set eyes on Hope Jennifer Richardson. I was totally mesmerized by her words – frozen - and my eyes fixed themselves on the wall just one metre in front of me focusing on the detail - the paintings and their alignment one with another.

I went back to other room to be met with enquiring eyes. I felt an extraordinary sense of elation when Mrs Hathaway added that my face was familiar, that there was something about the shape of my face - I looked like Jennifer - and she touched the contours of her own with her fingertips as she spoke.

The thing is, an adoptee has never had a mirror image of looking like anybody, anybody at all. The gap that probably most adoptees would like to fill, even the ones who don't want to find their genetic roots, is the, 'who do I look like?' It feels *normal* to not look like anyone, and so it is the oddest feeling, when a connection, however obscure, presents itself. While others take their family similarities for granted, we can only take the opposite for granted: that we are *not* connected by genes to anyone we know, we are like nobody. I have read in books that it has been likened to a floating feeling - no roots holding us to the ground, no moorings, no foundation - that we weren't really born of anyone, we just sort of arrived on planet Earth somehow. That is in fact exactly how it feels.

Much later in this process, while I was waiting for my DNA results to arrive, I imagined the nice receptionist at the end of the phone saying, "Mrs Miceli, I'm terribly sorry, but your results are most unusual: we cannot assess your DNA as it appears to be non-existent." These words would not have surprised me.

You see, when a baby is born into a family, the very first comments are about similarities: 'Awww, he's so like his uncle Pat…', 'Isn't he the splitting image of his father?' 'She's got her grandmother's red hair.' The comments continue throughout her life. They are like markers, reminding the child who she is. Even 'She's so *unlike* any of us,' ironically still reinforces who she is. Simply because it's a *surprise* that she's different. Of course for the adoptee, the difference is *natural.*

The un-adopted knows, from a genetic point of view, what she is supposed to be like: physically, emotionally, intellectually. However she develops, she is still the right person – herself, with her rightful identity, whatever shape and form that might be. One might say that this is true too for an adoptee: whoever you are or however you become is right.

But for lack of mirror images and past connections, she actually doesn't know the right self because she has no base to work from. She has to invent it from the inauthentic mirror image of her adoptive parents.

That invention can never be the right one for she is never going to be the child of their genes. My parents made the grave and misguided error of thinking that they should not tell Finn that his mother was an accomplished musician and scholar, because it might pressure him to be good in music. If only they had realized that any small piece of information that we were given would be welcome. We would have clung to any information like limpets, just as I did to the name Jane, because something instinctive inside of us told us that it was important, that it meant something, even if we knew not what. I too was told absolutely nothing of either my birth mother of father or grandparents' accomplishments. Later in my search, I discovered letters around my adoption, which disclosed this information. All the time, my parents knew.

So however much love adoptive parents can give - and many give copious quantities and undoubtedly make their child feel loved – they can only offer an *acquired* identity – the authentic genetic identity remaining a mystery. There is no genetic past for her, no genetic history for her to hold onto.

As an adoptee, then, my history was an 'invention' - history and roots handed on plate with names, labels, stories, but with ancestors who genetically had nothing to do with me at all. I have an exquisite collection of family silver with dates and poignant family crests, or initials. It is an odd thought that when they were made or bought for the Quinn-Smiths, the Agars, the Murrays, the Banners, who would have ever guessed that they would end up in my tender hands. Now I find it a sweet thought that these precious objects will start on a new journey, all because of me.

Of course I couldn't be certain that I was connected to the Akehursts. I would just have to wait until either Mrs Henderson or Mrs Hathaway contacted Jennifer. That's how we'd left it.

After having got the children to bed that same evening, sitting eating my supper, the phone rang. It was 9 o'clock. I heard Alan say, "You may. I'll just call her. Who's speaking please?"

I knew who it was before the caller had time to tell Alan his name.

It was Quentin Akehurst for me.

It was exciting but terrifying. I began with an apology about poking around in Worpleston and asking about his family. I didn't mean to pry, I just really wanted to find my birth mother and understand who and where she was.

"Hope is my first cousin. And *you, you* are the baby who has been missing in all these years, and in our lives. We have been waiting for this moment. Waiting and hoping, and now here you are! At last we've found you! We have *missed* you," he stressed the 'miss' part. "You're the missing baby! Our missing baby."

I don't know who was more incredulous, he or I.

I'd been preparing myself for rejection, both consciously and unconsciously. I had been concerned in an obscure way about how my birth mother would see me - not want me - and therefore how anybody who might be connected to her would see me too. This man *was* connected to her. But none of my self-defensive preparations were in the least necessary.

He was opening his arms to me.

"I don't know what to say." I replied.

CHAPTER TWENTY

"Quentin, I have to tell you something." Mrs Hathaway had said to Quentin over the telephone after Rosemary and I had left. "Two women were here today asking about you and your family." She had been about to proceed with her story, but Quentin had interrupted her: "You don't need to explain. I know who she is."

They had never been able to tell anyone, but had always known about Hope's baby. Now he could tell Mrs Hathaway the story.

"Well you must call Catriona straight away, Quentin, and put her out of her misery. She needs to know who she is! Don't keep her waiting a moment longer." Mrs Hathaway was an adoptive mother herself.

And this is how Quentin had come to call me that evening.

Although I'd already discovered through the village that the Akehurst family were Canadian, and that Quentin was the youngest son, I now learned on the telephone, that Peter Akehurst, his father, was the elder brother of Hope's mother, Eleanor. Hope too was Canadian then, and lived in Canada with a family of her own. Apart from her spell with the Akehursts in 1965, she had never lived in England.

"Oh, I see," I said, "but why were you and your family living in England then?"

Eileen and Peter had made the decision to leave Montreal at the end of the 50s, and emigrate to England. Neither of them felt comfortable in the affluent area of Montreal where they and Peter's family lived. They found the lifestyle superficial and false. Appearances were all- important – what you wore, what you said, who you knew, who you married – all of this *mattered* terribly. Not to Peter or Eileen, but very much so to his sister Eleanor, to their parents and their parents' friends.

As a small child in the twenties, Peter had contracted Scarlett Fever and was left almost stone deaf. This in itself made him different. His deafness went undetected by his parents who thought him retarded and treated him as such. It was not until he was eight that they realized what had happened. But crucially the way they treated him never deviated. I was listening and trying to take it all in. It wasn't about Hope though.

Quentin described his father to me. "He didn't care at all about what the neighbours would think, you see. Actually he became rather eccentric and he shouted a lot because of his deafness. They found him embarrassing really – I mean his sister Eleanor, his parents, his aunt. He just wasn't like them. Then he married Eileen, my mother, and they decided to move away from all that and come and live in England. In the end they settled in Worpleston you see, and never looked back. So that's why."

And Hope?

Ten years later or so, Hope, Peter's niece, found herself in a similar predicament: she too was an embarrassment to the family – she was pregnant and unmarried.

"That's why *you* were born in England! You were born here because of us."

Hope's mother Eleanor had married Thomas Richardson a doctor, also from Montreal. Hope was their second child, one of five. Quentin told me that Thomas and Eleanor decided to send her to stay with Peter and Eileen – her aunt and uncle in England, where she could have the baby, give it up for adoption, come back to Canada after an appropriate amount of time and no one would ever know.

"But my parents wanted to adopt you themselves, you know. They just found it outrageous that you should be given away. They couldn't bear it and wanted at least that you remained in the family, even if not with Hope." I felt something I couldn't quite identify – something good – as I gripped the receiver. "They tried persuading Hope's parents, but Thomas and Eleanor wouldn't hear of it. I think the words Thomas used were, 'a clean break'; yes, he was the decider as far as I know. So tragic. My parents were devastated. In fact they were the ones who had to take you to the agency I think it was, and give you away. It wasn't Hope herself."

Since the Akehursts lived in England and the Richardsons in Canada, the two families never really saw one another and Quentin didn't really know Hope. Eileen had only got to know her when she stayed with them that year. They knew Virginia, Hope's sister, better.

"Virginia has always known about you. In fact when we sold Scribbins in Worpleston and moved to Yorkshire, she was really concerned." Quentin explained.

"About what?"

"Well, she was very worried that the baby, *you,* would be unable to trace her origins if we sold the house."

This was all so much to take in. Yet he still had not told me anything about Hope. Where did she live? Was she married? Did she have any children? What was she like?

"She lives in Vancouver and has two boys."

"What do you think she'll think? Hope I mean? Will she be pleased I've found her? Did she want to look for me?"

"I really can't say I'm afraid. I know that Jennifer could never ask her – it was such a forbidden topic, a secret not to be talked about. Hope's sister Virginia told Jennifer that Hope didn't want to find you – she'd "put it all in the past". It's impossible to know how Hope will react to this."

"Oh," was all I could say.

I'd never imagined she might not want to find me. Now I felt confused – I was trying to correlate the mother I'd dreamed of - the mother who dreamed of finding me, longing for the day she would be re-united with me - and *this* information, this news. I couldn't yet - certainly not so suddenly - transform my long-held dreams into anything different – this reality. What *was* this reality? All was separate, disjointed.

What had not been a part of my make-believe though, was the existence of other people in her family, and in this case, other people who would want to find me.

We talked for about forty minutes. When I put down the telephone, the feeling of gratitude was almost overwhelming. I was grateful I wasn't being rejected. I was elated that I was being welcomed in.

"…My father, I remember my mum saying, apparently wrote to his sister saying that pride was a much worse sin than lust (he was a very religious man,) and that therefore it was worse for them to send Hope away to save the scandal, than it had been of her to conceive you…." These were some of the words written by Ben, Quentin's elder brother, in a letter to me just the next day. Then Jennifer telephoned. They were *all* involved. *All* so excited, so moved. It was a dream. My dream.

When they told Eileen that I had been found, she cried. I met her some weeks later, I asked her, "Did you ever imagine this? I mean that one day I might come looking?"

"No. When I handed you over, I thought I'd never see you again."

The next day, Saturday, I went to Brighton with the children to stay with my friend Lalli as had been planned. My mind was whirling and I allowed myself to enjoy the idea of these new people - real people, real cousins. They weren't her – Hope.

For now I could put off the 'moment of truth' a little while longer. I was happy in this state; it gave me time to breath, some space to brace myself for facing her, for making myself acceptable to her.

Quentin phoned again. He wanted to come and meet me. I don't know who was more excited. We could meet in Brighton the next day, Sunday 18th July 2004, my birthday.

Early, 8.30am, he rang again. Hope, he said, was about to telephone me. She would call me now, before I was to meet him. I had half an hour to prepare myself. She was furious, he'd told me. Furious he was coming to meet me.

I was terrified.

Just then the phone began ringing. I stared at it sitting there on Lalli's desk, ringing away in its own innocuous fashion, it, oblivious to the reaction its loud *dring dring* sound was causing inside of me. I now feared her. Not just her possible rejection of me - now there was her displeasure to contend with. Lalli and Norman were urging me to pick it up.

I did.

"Hello?"

"Can I speak to Catriona please?" a soft very feminine voice pronounced my name correctly – Catrina.

"Hope?" I answered.

"Yes."

"Hope, my mother Hope?"

"Yes, I'm your mother Hope."

"You mean you're my mother, my real mother, Hope? You're actually her? You are Hope. Hope Richardson on my birth certificate? That's you who I'm talking to?" Came my voice. I couldn't help repeating myself. It couldn't be real. Her voice. Her.

"Yes I am." Came the reply, lightly, with a smile I think, and a sort of 'cuckoo' lilt, on the 'am'.

I felt numb. Amazed not just that I was hearing her voice for the first time, but more that she was hearing mine. That I was in her mind in that precise moment. It made me feel honoured, like speaking to a favourite star, a hero. And what on earth would she be thinking of me? An imposter, an invader of her privacy. What could I say to not displease her? To keep her. I stood there clutching the phone to my ear, hanging on her every word, preparing myself to not be accepted.

I spoke. I began to try to put right what I thought had angered her. I apologized for being so determined to find her. I apologised about the way in which I had managed to do so - through the Akehursts. I apologised for it being such a shock to her. I finished by saying that I'd been wanting to find her for the greater part of my adult life and that I'd been thinking about her forever.

123

"It's not your fault," she replied, "it's just that everything is coming out too fast. It's like there's a tap turned full on and I'd like to turn it down a bit. I'd like a little more control and I feel I have none."

I understood. I'd had all my life to prepare myself, I told her. I could see how shocking it must be to have it all thrown at her, in just one day.

"But it's *you* I'm looking for. It's you. It's always been about you. You're the one. I've thought about you all my life, and now I've found you." I said. "Quentin is just a stepping-stone. But it is you who is my goal." I finished.

What did I hear in her voice? Was it surprise perhaps? Or was it gratitude? I'm not sure. She changed.

"Well I hear it's your birthday." *She didn't know it was my birthday?* "So you should do what you want. If you want to go and meet Quentin, then you have my permission."

"Well thank you," I replied, feeling, yes, gratitude - gratitude that it was ok by her for me to meet Quentin. I absolutely must not do anything that would displease her.

I might lose her.

Oddly, she didn't seem to know which year she had had me either. "I was just trying to work it out with Richard. I must have been either 1964 or 1965."

"It was 1965," I informed her.

We changed course. She asked me what I looked like. I was sporty wasn't I? Well, no not really. I wasn't particularly good as sport. Oh, because we're all very sporty. And you're thin aren't you. I confirmed. And you have a longish face and brown hair don't you. That's your father. Yes that too. On it went, our heights and anything we could think of - my green eyes. Yes we both had green eyes and freckles. The conversation lightened up and started to become fun. We laughed. She even told me my father's name.

"Your father's name is Fraser. Fraser Cawthorn. He's very good looking, or was as I remember him. Tall, with brown hair," and she recounted something about her and her husband Richard selling their house in Toronto and a connection with Fraser's mother and knowing the family. Then there was something about Fraser's ex-wife's house being in their same street.

It went in one ear, but not quite out the other. I was mildly curious about him in that moment - perhaps I was interested in what he looked like but no more - not who he was. How can you take in all this information about more than one person at a time? You would need two brains. In that moment, I formed an unfocused image of 'the boy who got her pregnant'. It didn't occur to me to match the 'boy' with, 'my father' - a part of me.

We talked on. I made reference to my children, and this produced an audible intake of breath, as if it were something unexpected but then suddenly realized all in the same moment. *You have three grandchildren* I'd said. It's always easy to talk about your children. I mentioned my wedding and when I'd got married. I could almost feel her eyes opening, like she was having a series of mini surprises, one after another – Oh she's done *that* and *that* - so many things have happened.

There was just so much she didn't know.

Everything.

We left it that we would e-mail one another. I felt grateful. Grateful that she would like to reconnect. And relief. All would not be lost when I put the phone down. I didn't have to be frightened of letting the conversation go. There would be another. I would hear from her again. We had a beginning.

Standing there in my pink pyjamas, Lalli and Norman teary-eyed looking on, I felt dazed. Star-struck. It was hard to realize that the person with whom I'd just been talking was Her - my Mother - flesh and blood. Yet I had just discovered a problem: she wasn't one and the same as the mother I'd kept secretly in my mind for all these years – that imaginary person, that ghost of her – *that* mother was still more real to me. I just couldn't make the connection. Who was this stranger? The ghost I knew. I couldn't bridge the gap.

I fear I never have.

Monday morning, I found myself driving off again, three children in tow, not back to base – the Willis's - but back to the village of Worpleston, my birth place. I had been invited by Mrs Hathaway to have lunch at her house. Quentin was staying there.

Events of the past three days had made history, my history. I was changing. I remember walking along a street in Brighton over that weekend staying with Lalli and realizing, that for a certain number of hours, I had not thought of Finn.

Now in the car, I was no longer approaching an unfamiliar village with trepidation. The anticipation of being met with suspicion that I had felt, when reaching Lark's Rise, Mrs Hathaway's cottage for the first time, felt an eternity away. This time, I was an invited guest.

Just as the rooms in the house from our childhood can be mesmerizingly different – shrunken -after decades of having not seen them through our adult eyes, so did Lark's Rise with its gate, its path, its front door, look different this time. In only three days it had changed from an anonymous cottage to a friendly home ready to welcome me in.

It was one of those rare warm sunny English summer days, the children, feeding off my happiness, were easy, comfortable, and I too felt comfortable in my printed cotton dress and red sandals. As we walked along the path outside the cottage which lead to the garden behind, we followed my new-found cousin Quentin, I noticed on the corner, the buddleia waving its graceful purple heads of flowers welcoming me. Then we were in her charming English garden set slightly on a slope with an apple tree and a swing. We sat on her flagstone patio, Mrs Hathaway, Quentin, myself and the children, eating roast chicken going over and over the events, laughing and joking until we had run them dry.

It was only now, even after having spent the whole day before with my new cousin, that I actually noticed him, I mean really took him in, the fact of him. I found myself studying him. Half turned from me, not quite a full profile I looked at him - tall, good looking. There appeared a familiarity to me and I was deaf to any sound, because for the first time since meeting him, it began to dawn on me, like an ice cube just beginning to melt, that this person was connected to me by blood, by genes, the first person ever, and the birth of this thought took up all of my senses such that there was room for nothing else.

CHAPTERR TWENTY-ONE

Nobody can warn you what to expect when you find your birth mother. You can read all the manuals you like, but no amount of preparation can tell you what you will really feel when you actually set eyes on her. There is only one way to find out.

The date was set for 25th August. The month that passed by between that first conversation with her, and our first meeting was a whirlwind. No day was the same. I was in a balloon, which I feared would pop at any moment. There was also no time to consider properly what was happening or to review my feelings.

After the momentous first call, and after my meeting with Quentin, Hope had got upset again. She, from her long distance in Canada, put a stop to any more meetings with the Akehursts. 'This isn't working for me', she wrote.

It didn't occur to me that I too could express what was or wasn't working for me.

Now I was so enjoying the feel of the Akehursts, but I wasn't allowed to see them. I didn't understand. I did as she requested and did not go to meet Eileen or the rest of the family. She had never asked how I felt.

My children and I returned to Italy towards the end of July. There were e-mails that flew in all directions, with photograph attachments, phone calls, not just with her. We were all talking about it, and I was under my own spell of elation. I had found my missing mother.

She sent me only one photo. In 2004 attached photos didn't open up instantly – chunks of image appeared slowly, oh so slowly. I couldn't tear myself away and come back later to see the full-blown picture, but as I sat and waited, no amount of staring at the picture could hurry it up.

At first I could only see a blur of colours, then a part was becoming hair, then skin, then teeth but it was an eternity before she was there, whole.

I stared glued. How much time passed before my mind could register her – her face, her look, her expression? A split second perhaps. Or maybe more. Then she was smiling, her head half turned to the person beside her.

But as I continued to stare, I became shocked. She was so different from what she was supposed to look like. She was supposed to look like me! I couldn't see me in her at all. Where was my mirror image? I examined every inch of her face. My own smile was not there, her teeth looked different from mine, her ear lobes weren't mine, nor the way my ears finish in a point at the top; she didn't have my pointed chin or line of my jaw. The whole shape of her face was different. Her hair fell differently and did not frame her face the way mine did and besides, she was blond. This couldn't be my mother. In her place was an attractive smiling woman but the lack of connection that was I was expecting to both see and feel, gave way to disappointment.

Then there was her voice that by now I had heard many a time on the end of the telephone. I couldn't synchronize the face in the picture, with the voice. I liked the voice but it was so separate, separate from the face and separate too from the words on the screen in the e-mails. The printed words belonged to one, the photo another, and the voice here on the telephone yet another. All segmented, disjointed. She had three facades and none of them, not even the least direct – that of the e-mails - was the right one.

Besides her different and confusing facades, there was a strange lack of logic in her words; not in how or in what she was saying - she expressed herself perfectly well - but something didn't add up: the meaning behind her words bore no resemblance to what I had always imagined her to think and feel, just as the photo of her had not resembled me as I had imagined it would.

In an early conversation when I was still at the Willis's' she was talking about her parents. They were still alive. Her mother had advanced Alzheimer's, but her father, at eighty-five, was still very alert. She talked highly of him, his achievements as a surgeon, of how he was loved and looked up to by all, but it surprised me that she was so concerned about upsetting him in telling him that I had found her.

"So how do you feel about your parents?" I asked.

I imagined she loathed them and that she would have fallen out with them a long time ago. You see, I had considered them the ones responsible for my adoption, especially having heard the Akehursts' account, and had therefore automatically assumed that *she* held them responsible too, hating them for what they'd done to her and to me. I imagined always that she had never in her wildest dreams actually *wanted* to give me away. No, she herself had loved me forever but her parents had wrenched me away from her forcing her into a state of despair and anguish. I saw no other possibility.

"Oh, I am very close to my parents," she replied proudly. "I love them both dearly. I have a very special relationship with my father in particular," said affirmed, with the tone of assumption that this was something I would enjoy hearing.

You don't always realize when something hurts. Sometimes there's just an inner suspicion. I sat there in the hall at the Willis's, taking in this conflicting information and trying not to let it trouble me.

She went on to say that she hadn't known how or when to tell her father about my appearance in her life, because she was concerned about upsetting him. However, when she did manage to tell him, his immediate reply had been, '*you must go to her then!*'

I was unnerved again. It was as if she sat at the foot of his pedestal, treating his words like an emperor's proclamation. Where were *her* feelings about me? Where were *her* thoughts of wanting to '*go to me*'?

And then how was it possible that she not only didn't despise her father, but also positively revered him? The last few words of a later e-mail from her impressed this upon me yet further:

Sunday 1st August 2004

"*Oh and the other news is that, there was a small family dinner at my parent's country home where they now permanently live. On the dining room table are all your photos I had. Dad is already showing them around to my brother and his daughters, saying 'look at my granddaughter', while I am still wondering whether it would be just a little too much for my poor Dad to swallow. What a laugh. Not at all, he seems genuinely thrilled. My dear Mum, unfortunately simply will not able to grasp it all. Now all your aunts and uncles and cousins know and love the whole excitement of it. If my father blesses it, then all is well! So you are on the map!*'

'*If my father blesses it, then all is well!*' the words rang in my head.

It was in this conversation that she expressed her desire to meet me.

CHAPTER TWENTY-TWO

The date of our meeting approached.

Lorenzo and I arrived at the airport in Rome on Thursday 25th August 2004 at 2pm. We stood, Lorenzo and I, looking at faces and waited, surreally calm.

Out came a stream of people. Which one was she? That one with the red suitcase? Maybe that one over there looking for someone? No, she wasn't through yet.

"There she is!" said Lorenzo.

"Where?"

"There, look, with the short blond hair. That woman facing the other way. No, look!! She's walking the other way. It's her." His tone was sure, definite.

"No, That's not her."

"Yes it is. It's her. Can't you tell?"

A woman with short straight-cropped blond hair. But Lorenzo was mistaken. This person was a far a cry from the right one. This was a nameless traveller just like any other, not the one that I was looking for.

Lorenzo was continuing to point at her insisting. I was in another place still looking for the right person. Seconds passed. It was becoming suspiciously apparent that Lorenzo was right because she was walking towards me. This was her. I wanted it to be another person walking towards me, not this person.

I was taking her in and at the same time, struggling. S*he* was wrong. This woman was dressed very nicely, appropriately, bright eyed, smiling, questioning, but it was still all wrong. Was it that she looked too *un*like me to be my mother? Where was the older version of *me*? She was like a girl too – not a mother, not *my* mother! And yet she looked more or less the age she was – fifty-eight. She looked good in fact. But where was my '*Mother*'? She wasn't physically big enough for a start - she was *my* size! My mother had to be physically bigger than me, surely? One able to embrace, embrace all her brood, hold them all, all her beloved children, the lost and the found. Yet she was petite and slim - sporty looking, brisk. And her hair - it was supposed to be gentle and curving slowly down to her shoulders, but here was only bluntness, a severing at the neck.

She walked closer. I stood waiting. Now she was in front of me and I was putting my arms around her and we were touching and embracing. We pulled back to take a look at one another - her eyes full of glee - and she told me I was beautiful. We looked. We laughed. Lorenzo was in awe and his only words were about our eyes. How we had the same eyes.

But I couldn't see it. She had. She had seen the connection the moment she saw my photograph a month before and had stressed often how similar I was to her. I tried. I looked for me in her eyes but I couldn't find myself.

We sat in the back of the car together and she gave me her ring. It was like a signet ring, gold, with initials engraved. Her sister had told her to give it to me, she said. I spent the rest of the journey in cloud of dumb amazement. I expect she felt the same.

We arrived back on our farm three hours later. I offered her a cup of tea. She sat in the armchair opposite me, and for an instant, expressed not just amazement, but something more: she was incredulous that she was looking at her own flesh and blood, her daughter.

It *is* that amazing. In your numb state, you just keep reminding yourself who this person is, because in fact you are looking at a total stranger.

I asked her about my birth. Memories of the births of my own three children were still quite recent, details of which were crystal clear, but when I listen to others' stories that might even be forty or fifty years old, I see their memories serve them equally well. I don't think a mother can ever forget.

Unless there has been a trauma of a particularly unusual kind.

I asked her what time she had me, what the labour was like, how easily or not easily I was born; all of it. I had to know.

She could remember having a bath there in the hospital. She couldn't remember the length of the labour or birth. She could remember something of the pain. She thought that it had been towards the end of the day.

"What did you feel as you looked at me? I mean did you love me as you held me in your arms?" Of course she did but I needed to hear her confirmation.

"Well, no." came her reply with raised eyebrows and a shrug. "No, I didn't feel anything. I do remember thinking it was a surprise that you had brown hair. You weren't blond like all of us, you see. But no, I didn't feel a thing. I think I was just an airhead. I'm sorry but I can't lie to you. I can't invent what wasn't true."

"Oh, that's ok," I said. "It's good you can tell me the truth," I replied, taking her answer in my stride.

"So why did you choose the name Jane?" Of course the name Jane was special to her.

"Well, I couldn't choose a name that *meant* anything to me you see."

The reason she'd chosen Jane was precisely because it had *no* meaning for her. As we sat in the two armchairs, that first day of meeting, she told me she remembered the nurse telling her that she had to give her baby a name - the baby must be registered.

"*Oh just call her Jane!*" She waved her hand now, flipping the back of it to the air imitating what she had done there in the hospital. "Just give her any old name. Call her Jane, that'll do, and be done with it." It had to be the plainest name possible she went on. "You know, Plain Jane, no connotation, no *connection* to me in any way. I mean I didn't want to choose a horrible name! Just a name that didn't *connect* me to you." She was insistent on this word 'connect'. It was this that would do her harm - the connection with me. It dawned on me that this was a measure of her love for me – the fact that she needed to *dis*connect, meant there was a connection – and for this I was grateful.

People told me that this was wrong – wrong of her – when I would recount the story behind my name. But they didn't get it. Hope had had a hard time – it must have been awful for her, but now I was her daughter, now I would be loved by her. We would make up for all that lost time.

During her stay, we showed one another photographs. She gave me ones of herself, of her two sons Joel and Konner, and a CD full of pictures of her whole family and their family home – where her parents still lived. There were pictures of everybody in her family. Hope has two brothers and one sister. All have their own children. All these people - names and faces – meant nothing to me. I felt no connection. I felt disinterested, unimpressed, by the pictures of these two half-brothers. Besides, Finn had only just died. I acted interested out of politeness and a sense of obligation.

I showed her pictures of my family and of the Micelis. I told of the tragedies – my brother's death, my mother and her tragic story, of Lorenzo's father's early death and of Giovanni, my sister in law Monica's little boy who had died at the age of seven. Hope was standing near the chest of drawers where I have so many photographs proudly on display.

"Can't you tell me something happy? This is all so negative and sad!"

I apologised. She didn't want to hear tragic stories.

There were moments during this first time with her, when she 'told all' - the truths about her life, her marriage. It was a letting go - revealing intimate or secret things about herself - just as we sometimes do when we meet a complete stranger, and tell them everything because we feel so free to do so. I lent a sympathetic ear.

She told me she'd felt like a nothing, with no self-respect. She'd never done well in school and had once had to repeat the year. She'd never had a real job or followed any kind of career or goal, nor excelled in anything even though she had been very good at sports. She had felt all her life that her parents thought her unintelligent, particularly her father. Many years before she had met Richard, she'd been madly in love with a young man who was also at McGill. His name was Joe; she'd adored him but he hadn't been very kind to her and the relationship didn't last.

"Did Richard know you'd had a baby?"

"Oh yes, I had to tell *him.*" Hope replied. "I mean, I could hardly not tell him could I?"

"Did you ever talk about it with him? I mean discuss the fact of me and stuff?"

"Nope." She replied simply. "We just never talked about it. He knew, but that's as far as it went. I just had to forget about you, you see. Virginia was the only person apart from my parents of course, who knew."

"Virginia called me as soon as she heard." I replied.

I had received a call from Hope's sister just two days after I had spoken to Hope. She had been so moved when she heard my voice, that for the first few moments, all she could do was weep. Tears of elation that I'd at long last been found.

"I know! The little wretch!" came Hope's angry words. "She would have to go and put her nose in it!"

But apart from telling her husband and her sister, she never told another living soul – not her brothers, not her sons, her secret locked away.

Locked away yes, but surely I remained within her heart all the time?

"Did you ever think about me? I mean didn't you ever wonder about me, where I was, what had become of me, if I was all right? Didn't you wonder what I looked like? I mean I so wanted to know about you and who you were and what you looked like."

"Well I do remember once sitting on my bed, and you floated into my thoughts. I recall thinking, 'I wonder if she's married now', but then I banished the thought, telling myself it would do me only harm to think of you." I pictured the bed, I pictured her, just as I had always pictured everything about her. I clung to the image – the image of *her* having a fleeting image of *me*.

I did long for more, and I know I tried to solicit some measure of regret from her, but it never came. "Oh 'guilt' is such a *useless* emotion," was what she said.

While she stayed the five days in our house, she commented on how wonderful it was that I could be so relaxed about managing my household. I found the comment strange. But she told me that she had always been, and still was, overly concerned about neatness and cleanliness. There was regret in her voice. She wished she could be like me. She had spent more time, she told me, during the boys' childhoods, cleaning and fussing around the house, than being with them and enjoying them. Everything had to look perfect. She admitted too that she could never enjoy food, not fully, because she was too busy considering its damage or indeed nutritional value. As well as this, she suffered bouts of intestinal cramps, which she resolved with medication, also from depression, and relentless insomnia. She did in fact go to see a psychologist when her pain became unbearable.

It didn't occur to her to tell her therapist that she'd had a secret baby – a baby lost in the past. She'd had *two* children, - two boys – with Richard. That was it.

CHAPTER TWENTY-THREE

During this first visit I became curious about my birth father and my conception. Until now, I had been entirely focused on my mother.

Who was he then, and did I remind her of him? I'd decided I must look like him.

"No," she said, "I can't really see him in you." I felt the surprise, a mild disappointment. Well, could she remember him? What happened?

"Oh yes, of course I can remember him! You must understand that everybody knew everybody in our neighbourhood. He lived just a few doors down on the same street. I told you his name didn't I?

"Yes, Fraser something wasn't it?"

"Fraser Cawthorn. Well I can tell you he was at McGill studying biochemistry. I know that. I had been invited to a fraternity party one evening. I do remember going upstairs with him and I know that I was lying there with him. I told you we didn't actually do it."

"*What?* No, you didn't tell me. What do you mean you didn't do it?"

"Well I told you I thought? I thought you'd understood?" She said fairly simply. Understood what? No I hadn't understood. What on earth was she talking about?

"I was a virgin you see. We were lying there together, and then right in that moment – he was *there*," and she indicated down between her legs, "but he wasn't *in*, and I thought, 'this can't be *it.* I don't want this'. I didn't want to lose my virginity to him you see. He wasn't anybody important to me. I changed my mind. So I said 'stop'."

"So what did he do?"

"Well he did. I mean stop. So we didn't actually do it you see!"

"No, that's not possible! So he wasn't my father? You're saying this?"

"He *is* your father! I *did* get pregnant like that. I didn't think I was, you see. I mean it was impossible. Then my period was late. But it didn't occur to me that I could be pregnant. Later, I lost my virginity to Joe. You know the one I was so mad about."

"Do you think Joe is my father?" Oh my goodness, I thought as visions of him flashed through my mind. A whole new person to think about.

"No, he's not. Joe is definitely not your father. It's Fraser. It *was* Fraser. I went to see the doctor some time later because my period still hadn't come and I was getting worried. And sure enough, the doctor confirmed I was pregnant."

Hope too in that moment had thought that it was Joe, but when the doctor told her it was far too late for an abortion – she was four months pregnant now – she realized the gruesome truth that she had got pregnant way before she'd even met Joe.

She knew then that it had been Fraser. Fraser was the father. My father.

It was astounding. Was it really possible you could get pregnant like that? I was conceived, not by two people making love but by two people *not* making love. A one in a million. On top of that, they barely knew each other. All my fantasies about a great, doomed love affair shattered.

I imagined her horror too. I could imagine her listening to the frightening news sitting there in the doctor's office, alone.

Westmount, Montreal. 1964. For a young unmarried girl to *get herself pregnant* (the expression itself implying it were a feat she could achieve all by herself), was shameful, a scandal, nice girls didn't do that. Nice girls were virgins.

Hope was in disgrace. Thomas and Eleanor Richardson had a very embarrassing situation that needed dealing with quickly. They needed to protect themselves and protect Hope. Hope barely knew Fraser Cawthorn and if she had the baby without being married to him, then her future would be ruined. Her father was becoming a renowned and respected surgeon, her mother, according to Hope, was the perfect wife, running the perfect family.

Her own sister, she said, cared nothing for social status, kept a very different group of friends, and would have kept her baby at all costs had it happened to her. But *Hope* wanted the approval of her parents. *Hope* enjoyed the company of wealthy boyfriends with the smart cars. And it was *Hope* who didn't want to give it all up, she told me, not wistfully at all. No, if she had wanted to keep the baby, she would have had to change her life. And she didn't intend to do *that*. She never told Fraser either.

"So what did you do?" I asked.

She told her mother.

However shocked Eleanor, her mother, might have been, she didn't show it. Unexpectedly, she sat Hope down on the bed and without anger or judgment said, "Now don't you worry. We will resolve this."

I pictured Hope sitting awkwardly with her mother with whom emotions were never shown, let alone discussed. I wondered how they could begin to share such a secret.

Hope's mother came up with a solution: The Akehursts! She could go and stay with the Akehursts, all the way over in England, away from Montreal and gossiping quick-to-judge friends. She would have the baby, which of course would be given up for adoption. She could then come home again, and no one would ever have to know. Fraser would never have to be told, nor his parents. Even Hope's brothers knew nothing of the pregnancy.

"But was it your mother who thought of this solution though? I mean, it was your mother who was sending you there?" I needed to confirm that she'd been forced to do this.

"Well, I think we both came up with it together. It was sort of a joint decision. It was a great relief. My mother was so sweet about it and I felt so grateful. I also remember my father putting me on the plane saying, 'Now if there's anything you need, you must let me know.' I remember that. I know he wanted the best for me." Hope needed to convince me what caring parents she had.

The whole episode – a gap of six months – was never mentioned in the family, ever again. Not until thirty-nine years later when I came along and unintentionally unveiled this, the hidden secret, the family scandal.

"So what was it like living with the Akehursts?" I asked.

She told me what a lovely time she'd had there. Eileen was the opposite of her own mother. She was so willing to talk about what you *felt* - if you ever wanted to talk about anything, or had any kind of problem little or small, she would just drop everything and sit you down to talk it through. It was so easy with her. She was wonderful. Always helping people. Hope in turn helped with the children who were then nine, six and two. Peter, the father, was deaf, eccentric, all embracing and honest. They were both loving and kind people.

"But didn't you and Eileen talk about the baby? You must have felt the baby by then? I mean didn't you discuss what would become of me?"

"No, I think if anything it was always more on a practical level and what it would be like, the birth and all that."

A few days before I was born, tragedy struck back in Montreal. Daniel, Hope's brother, the fourth out of five children, was killed in a car accident. He was sixteen. Eileen and Peter had received this information via telegram. They asked the doctor at the hospital where I was born, when they should tell Hope. He said that she should be told immediately and taken home straight away (home to the Akehursts) instead of staying the stipulated ten days in hospital.

So after only three days, Hope left the hospital, leaving me behind. That was lucky, she said, because she didn't have time to fall in love with me.

"So what *did* you feel?"

She couldn't remember. She couldn't remember walking out of the hospital. She couldn't remember being told about her brother. All she could remember was the colour of my hair, not feeling anything at the time as she'd held me, and the decision to call me Jane.

Five days later, I was driving Hope back to the Rome airport. This time it was the two of us alone in the car. We were going to spend the night together, sharing a room near the airport since she had an early morning flight.

As I drove, I told her more of my brother Finn and how hard the past year had been. She expressed sympathy.

"Did you ever think to come looking for me?" I asked.

"Well, I just assumed I wasn't allowed to. I mean I couldn't!"

"But wouldn't you have *liked* to?" In my mind she had always thought to.

"I just wasn't allowed to."

With the subject still lingering in the air between us, I dared ask if her mother had ever thought of me. Yes Eleanor, already a mother of five, *she* must have suffered my loss. I was her flesh and blood, her granddaughter. I pressed Hope to tell me.

"So what did your mother feel about me? The baby I mean. Do you think she felt the loss?"

"Oh, you have no *idea* how she worried about me!"

I was baffled. Had she misheard my question?

But no, she went on. "She was so worried because in those days when you were born, a mother who had just given birth, had to stay in hospital for ten days. She was so worried that I would fall in love with you, that I would have a terrible time parting from you - and that I would suffer. You must understand how caring my mother was."

As I gripped the steering wheel in confusion, I focused hard on the motorway ahead – the cars passing me in their oblivion - and I forced myself to be happy that my 'grandmother' had thought of my 'mother', and that I should feel sorry for her - my grandmother, that is - as did Hope, for the anxiety the whole episode had caused her.

CHAPTER TWENTY-FOUR

I have always kept in my bedside table drawer, special letters and drawings our children have done over the years. Since I can't bear to throw any of them away, it's getting rather stuffed full. Some of the expressions are so precious, so priceless. Particularly with their Italian phonetic spelling:

"You are a welli cood cood aingiol. I love you" (Tom) There's a picture of me – an angel.

Or: *"For Mummy. I tidied the house because you were strest up. I hope it will make you happy! From your best Camilla. The best mummy a doghter could have!"*

Then of course, there are all the notes, even essays almost, left out for Father Christmas:

"Caro Babbo Natale, i regali che mi hai dato l'anno scorso erano bellissimi. Oh oh oh!! Quest'anno mi potresti regalare: 'Pony Tutto Per Me'. Pantofole con il pelo rosa, e anche altri regali che se me li dai, sono bellissimi. Grazie from Anna [Dear Father Christmas, the presents you gave me last year were lovely. Oh oh oh!! This year, could you give me: 'Pony All For Me'. Slippers with pink fur, and other presents that if you give me, I know will be lovely. Thank you, from Anna]

"Caro Babbo Natale, Io ti voglio tanto tantissimo bene, e da quanto ti voglio bene vorrei vederti, ma non posso, senno rompe l'incantesimo, giusto? E tutte le sere del 24 dicembre puoi darmi cosa ti pare. Non ti chiedo niente. Tutto quello che mi hai regalato in questi anni mi è sempre piaciuto. Quindi non ti preoccupare. Il tuo Thomas." [Dear Father Christmas, I really love

you a lot, and I love you so much, I want to see you, but I can't as it would break the spell, right? And every evening of 24th December you can give me whatever you think best for Christmas I'm not asking you for anything. I have really liked everything that you have given me. So don't worry. From your Thomas.]

In his drawing Father Christmas stands with his sack, by our fireplace with all the details on and around it.

Year after year, we would wonder together how on earth he manages to get round the whole world in just one night, how he can eat so many biscuits and drink so much milk without bursting, how he really does squeeze himself down chimneys without getting dirty, or magically shrink like Alice to squeeze through letter boxes if you don't have a chimney, and how he can know all the languages of the world.

Years before, I would sit excitedly on Shelagh's bed, Finn on Nat's, pulling out surprise after surprise from our stocking. Some things were so obviously bought by my mother from shops in Salisbury - I'd seen her buying them with my own eyes - but it would never occur to me that anyone other than The Man himself - the mystery magical man with a beard and a red suit - had procured them himself and, more importantly, specially for me. He knew *me. He* knew my tastes, my needs. I had a personal relationship with him. I adored him so much I confess I used to pray to him.

The last item in the stocking, always a tangerine. The feel of it as I would put my fingers around it - this almost hallowed tangerine - marked the end of that year's ritual, and the beginning of the long three hundred and sixty five day wait, for the next.

So Lorenzo and I carried on the English tradition. Stockings are left out by our huge Tuscan fireplace. Once discovered first thing Christmas Day, they are ceremoniously carried to our bed, like a jewel on a velvet cushion being brought to a king, and deposited ever so delicately. And then the opening begins.

Italians don't do Christmas stockings. Stockings are for the Epiphany on 6th January where La Befana will leave sweets in a stocking to children if they have been good. The original story is that an old lady – Befana - loses both her baby girl and husband to disease. A poor and lonely widow for the rest of her life, her only comfort is an old doll that her baby girl used to play with. One night she is looking out at the night sky for The Star that she has heard about, that will lead to the new King. When the three wise men, and later the shepherds, pass by, inviting her to join their journey to the King, she declines, feeling herself too lowly. In the morning she changes her mind and decides she too will go, and will offer her most precious treasure as a gift – her baby's old doll. In this way the doll will bring joy to another baby and in turn to her. On her journey she loses sight of the star and never reaches her destination - the Christ child. So La Befana continues today roaming the world seeking him, looking in through windows at children, and then offering her doll to them instead. In this way, she can express her love for her lost baby.

Christmas 2004, Hope came to stay, with Richard, her two boys Joel and Konner for two and a half weeks. These three men were coming to meet me for the first time. I was a sister, a sister the boys never knew they had, and a stepdaughter to Richard.

We put them all in one of our apartments. At last they were about to arrive. Excited and nervous, I had put the confusing conversations I had had with Hope during the summer, behind me. A few months had passed now anyway. I could hardly expect her to love me straight away. In fact, I *was* lucky – she was coming all this way yet again to see me, and this time, bringing her family too. The honour was all mine.

They were driving up from Rome and I had prepared one of our holiday apartments for them – the biggest and the best. They had to have the best. I had checked and double checked everything – plates, cutlery, pans, and of course the bathrooms, plenty of towels – everything had to be spotless, and there had to be everything they needed. I gave more attention to details than I ever had with regular guests. Yes, it was perfect, I said to myself as I closed the front door. Inside, the Christmas tree I'd carefully decorated, a poinsettia on the table, crystal vases on their bedside tables, a single rose in each – one for Richard and one for Hope. And I'd made sure to put the heating on three days before – it would take this long for the house to warm up – never mind the expense – they must be greeted by a warm house. Yes it was welcoming – they would be pleased.

I heard the crunch of wheels over gravel. My heart leapt and I rushed outside to greet them, waving and smiling.

The big shiny car came to a halt. Doors began to open and slam shut one after the other. Hope first – a hug with her. Then Richard, bald, friendly, smiling and affectionately telling me we – he and I - deserved a hug from each other too. Nice. Then the boys. Two lanky, dishevelled, twenty-six and eight year old boys. I greeted them effusively. I was so excited – excited for them too - but they were oddly stiff – blank almost. Jetlag, of course. Both held their eyes wide - big sensitive eyes – looking at me straight on, honest. I was looking for myself but I couldn't find myself in either of them.

I gave them all lunch. I had prepared a huge pot of soup to last us two or three meals. We gathered round our kitchen table. What did we talk about? Their trip, the children. Before I could say jack knife, the soup was all finished! Goodness, they were hungry.

A week passed. All of a sudden food was draining away from my fridge, my cupboard, like water. Lorenzo and I cooked. If I asked one of the boys to lay the table, then they kindly would. Sometimes Hope helped me with the food preparation and that was nice.

Christmas was upon us. Hope had gone to great lengths to bring presents – lovely presents for all. The day before, on Christmas Eve, Richard asked, "Do you need anything Catriona? I'm going to Greve."

"Oh, I was going myself to pick up the turkey for tomorrow."

"Well I can get it for you. Just tell me where to go."

"Thanks. Can I give the money later?"

"Oh sure. Don't worry about that," came his reply.

On his return, I thanked him. "Now let me pay you for that," I said going to my wallet. "How much was it?"

"It was," and then he made a show of getting his wallet out of his pocket and finding the receipt and looking at it to tell me how much. "Forty-two euros."

As I handed him forty-five, he insisted on showing me the receipt. "Look, look, here!" he said pointing to the amount written. He wasn't cheating me.

"I believe you, I believe you!" I said as I handed him the money. "I don't have the exact amount, keep the change."

He took the money, put it in his pocket and indeed, kept the change.

Here we were again, this time seated around our huge table in our sitting room on Christmas Day. We have a lovely big room – typically Tuscan – which almost takes your breath away when you enter, with its spectacular high ceiling, and mighty beams. It's the place to be for Christmas – roaring fire – the place for family gatherings. Here we were, Lorenzo and I with our little family, joined with this new family – my family.

The telephone rang. Conversation hadn't been stilted exactly, but it wasn't relaxed either. I reflected later that there wasn't any laughter. They took themselves very seriously. This was not a time for joking. With Nat and Shelagh, who had certainly had their problems, there was always laughter. Shelagh could shudder up and down in silence, as mirth would take a hold of her. Tears would spill from her eyes even. But these people were formal with each other and it was clear that Richard was the boss.

"Ah yes, just a meenit. I go," said Lorenzo as he went to answer. He has never bothered with grammar.

Hope had already heard and was eagerly halfway up. "That'll be Dad." Her father.

As the rest of us sat chatting, Hope leant around the corner, phone to ear, her eyes asking me to come - it would be appropriate for me to go and wish 'my grandfather' a happy Christmas. But I couldn't. I didn't know why - there was something gluing me to my chair - and I simply remained seated.

While we could hear Hope going on with her father, Richard began explaining to the boys, why Hope hadn't kept me.

"Well you see, it would have been absolutely im*possible* for her to keep Catriona." He was looking at them – talking to them – not to me. "For one, *I* wouldn't have married her!" There was more than just a hint of scorn. "And for that, just think, you boys wouldn't have existed."

They didn't answer. They didn't look at me either.

Then they all got ill. One after the other. Colds, coughs.

"You should take some vitamins Konner, with that cold you've got," said Hope to her son. We were around the table again. "I saw them on top of the fridge – there," Hope gestured towards my kitchen.

"I can't find them."

"I finished them," I said to Hope. "Sorry!" My supply had been very quickly disappearing and it had irritated me, so I had hid what was left. It was then I realized how exhausted I was. Lorenzo too. How little they were helping.

The days – all eighteen of them – dragged by. I was beginning to get frustrated. Lorenzo and I began a countdown to their departure.

"I'm just going to get a bottle of wine to take back to Canada," said Joel on the last evening before they left, letting himself into Lorenzo's winery and helping himself.

Finally, their car was crunching along the gravel, this time, in the opposite direction.

I felt the weight on my shoulders suddenly lift.

CHAPTER TWENTY-FIVE

I met my grandfather just a few months later. He was coming to stay with Hope for ten days, something he did every winter. This year Hope was orchestrating our meeting. It would be my first time in Hope's home, and in fact in Canada. She was very keen for her father to meet me.

If truth be told I was rather anxious about our meeting – all her descriptions of him were superlative. What would he think of *me*? I knew he had been a successful and well-known surgeon in Montreal all his life. According to Hope he had always excelled. How would I measure up?

He had insisted on coming with her to the Vancouver airport to meet me. I saw him standing behind the airport ribbon which divided the space between us, looking out for me along with Hope. He greeted me warmly.

"I'm your grandfather!" he said – positive, cheerful, optimistic. It was all very simple. He was eighty-five then but not old looking at all. Short but not hunched, slim, smiling, he was quite the opposite of tyrannical or commanding. At that moment I saw a resemblance; I saw my profile and recognized my nose and made my own mental note.

Getting into the car, he insisted on my taking the front seat. I was just about to get in the back. But he made it very clear that the best had to be for me, so for as long as the journey lasted from airport to home, I was his guest of honour.

Hope had other ideas. She tried to persuade him to not be so silly and come and sit in the front. The same again when we reached her home, and she showed me to the guest room where I was to sleep. It had a spectacular view over the ocean with a bay window. "It is perfect." I said. Hope lowered her voice: she *simply couldn't understand why* my grandfather had insisted on giving it up for me. He had wanted to move from this room up a few steps to a sofa-bed in the back room, with a view of the road. If it were up to Hope, this would be my room.

"Well, Catriona," again in the same cheery tone, "when are you going to come and stay with me in the Laurentians?" We were at dinner along with Richard, Joel and Konner.

Conversation was easy. Uncomplicated. I told him about our farm and he seemed genuinely interested. He gave me his complete attention. If I had been looking for his approval, it was clear that I had got it.

After my grandfather had had left, Hope and I were sitting one morning in her kitchen, a glass crystal kitchen table between us, with the stunning ocean view behind a wall of spotless glass. We were talking about Eileen and Peter Akehurst, her aunt and uncle, and her stay with them when she was going to have me. She was describing the way in which they were different from her parents.

I glanced around me. In Hope's house every surface gleamed, from the brand new red counter tops in the kitchen, to the 'touch screen' glass topped stove, the classic and gleaming antique furniture, bathroom and kitchen spotless. Nothing randomly left on any surface, only specifically placed ornaments with a purpose, no newspapers left on a table, no a mug in the sink. A vast off-white carpet that ran through the house, and the glass crystal kitchen table was wiped meticulously after any meal. On one occasion Hope told me I would find a hairdryer in her bathroom in the cupboard below the basin. It was a 'His and Hers' bathroom – I opened the wrong side - his - and was mesmerized. The temptation was to move one item just a millimetre to spoil the perfection. Even the ear cleaners in their box were perfectly in order, untouchably straight, not to be taken out at random.

"Eileen was wonderful. She had that way about her, you know – made you feel understood. For me it was a revelation – so new to me! In my family, we never '*talked*'. My mother wasn't like that at all."

I remembered Fiona, my own mother-friend, when I was sixteen, and how Shelagh seemed stuffy beside her.

Now, some twenty years later, it occurred to me, that Hope probably felt a little like I had, staying with Fiona at the same influential age. Her eyes must have been opened like mine, to a new sort of motherliness.

"Didn't you find yourself irritated by your mother when you got back? I mean returning to your mother who was so unreachable. Didn't she annoy you?"

"Oh no, Not at all! I was so *grateful* to her for helping me out you see. They had resolved my problem for me," she stressed.

A few days later, she took me to Whistler, their second home in the mountains. Here they could ski all winter and play golf all summer. Richard, having sold his business, didn't need to work any more. In the car, just the two of us, I asked, tentatively, "It's just rather strange, don't you think, that you are here with me now, so glad and happy, and so thrilled to have me in your life, and yet you don't seem to have any regrets about not having had me all these years?"

I can hear her answer as I write these words, the sing-songy intonation, its utter simplicity, just four words and a shrug.

"Well, I just don't."

Konner came to visit us there too. His friend Courtney came by one evening.

"So what age were you, Hope, when you had your first baby?" Courtney was thinking of having a baby in the near future.

Hope reflected a moment. "I was thirty. Yes about thirty." She was sitting opposite me on the sofa, I on the floor in front of her.

"No you weren't, Mum. How old were you when you had Catriona? Weren't you eighteen or something?" said Konner who, glancing first at me, turned towards her.

"Oh, *that!* Yes, sure, when I had Catriona I was seventeen, eighteen."

She couldn't remember that there are in fact twenty years between Hope and me.

Eventually I did go and stay with my grandfather at his home in the Laurentians the following year and again the year after that. It was a beautiful house set beside a lake. Remote too – I felt like I'd come to the middle of nowhere.

The first evening I arrived, Hope, who was there too, was standing just inside the bedroom where I was sleeping. It was a nice room upstairs, overlooking the driveway. It had been my grandfather himself who had insisted on bringing me up to show it to me - where the bathroom was and how to turn on the shower – it was he who wanted to explain to me the workings of the electric blanket, the ample cupboard space, the light switches, the thermostat on the wall, and advise me at what temperature to keep the room at night. There was his undisguised pleasure for all to see, about my arrival.

Once he'd left the room, I could tell there was something she was very keen to tell me.

"It was so funny! He just couldn't understand why you couldn't have the main guest bedroom. He was being so insistent that you should have the best room with your own bathroom and the view of the lake. I had to explain to him, 'No Dad, *I'm* the mother, *she's* the daughter. *I'm* first, *she's* second. The daughter has the green room! *I* have the pink room.' It was so cute the way he just couldn't understand that! We'd almost had a fight about it, until he eventually succumbed. Poor Dad, I don't think he was very happy about it!" She chuckled as she told it and I laughed along with her, agreeing on how sweet that was.

The second time I went, I arrived the day before her. He was so interested in everything I had to say, about my life and work back in London, my move to Italy, Lorenzo, my family, our farm and business, the children. He made pertinent comments and treated me with respect. Before supper we sat in his drawing room, which looked out on the lake, with a drink and nuts - not unlike the way Nat and I used to do back in my home in England - when I'd ask him about the war, or his medical career or his family.

He showed me upstairs as he liked to do, but this time, it was evident that he felt embarrassed about something. Hope had telephoned the day before to say that she was to have the best room - the pink room with the bathroom - and I the other.

As we stood in the doorway of the pink room, neither of us daring to enter, he suggested I move on in all the same before she got there – he so clearly wanted me to have it - but I laughed and said I wouldn't want to upset Hope's sleeping arrangements.

CHAPTER TWENTY-SIX

It was around this time that my father Nat died. I felt nothing. The drama of Nat was over and the door could be closed. My Mum was gone, Finn was gone, now the last threads to my past were gone too. Hope had been insistent that when he died, she would come with me to England, so that I would not have to face it alone.

She recognized that I was alone and referred to it several times - my life in England she said, "like a single ship roaming the seas waving the Richardson flag." That she, or her parents, had anything to do with my "sailing" there alone for all those years, never found its way between her lines.

At any rate, she did come to England and I was able to show her my home where I'd grown up, my home town, and even go for the same country walk I had done a thousand times before ever knowing who she was. That was nice. But with no other family member left, I did have to deal with Nat's death and its aftermath myself – picking up his belongings from the hospital, paying his nursing home bills, deciding what to keep of what he had had there, and where to put it (most I just took to the charity shop), and deciding which coffin to have, his cremation and when, and the announcement in the paper, and, later, the lawyer, the will and the rest. There's a lot to do when somebody dies, and burdensome to do alone. But I had no choice and Hope was there giving me support, which I appreciated enormously.

We stayed in a hotel together for five days. She accompanied me to the various places I needed to go to, and all the while, we talked.

As we walked down a pretty street in the medieval town of Salisbury, my home town, I said that Lorenzo and I would like to be able to buy a house in England, maybe around here.

"Oh, you're still looking backwards." she said knowingly.

I realized that she regarded my father's death as the point at which I should release myself from the 'chains of the past' – my home, my family, my life in England. Clearly she didn't understand who I was: my childhood, my education, my upbringing, Finn, Shelagh, Nat, were stories to be put away? She was waiting for me to land in her arms so that we could begin a new journey together, not at the beginning, but at a convenient spot somewhere in mid-air. She had *moved on* from my 'birth episode', and focused on our future. I on the other hand was slow, slow in 'getting there', stuck in the past. She had 'got over it' I must too.

"My parents too were blind," I said, "living by all those society rules. I mean they weren't able to see or understand what was truly right or wrong for Finn, for me. They just followed the rules. Know what I mean? Perhaps your parents were like that too, unable really think about the little baby growing inside of you?"

She turned on me then. Her eyes flared and she shouted, "BUT YOU WEREN'T EVEN BORN!"

I became her unborn child for a few seconds. I had no words to defend myself. I couldn't speak.

I turned and stalked away from her, barging into the hotel knowing she was following behind. For all I cared the swinging doors could hit in her in the face.

The following winter was our first visit as a family to Canada, to Hope's. By now, all of them had stayed with us including Joel, my half-brother, who had come to live with us in Tuscany for three months.

Now though, it was our turn to accept the offer and go with the children to stay with them in Vancouver and on to Whistler. Hope said she was longing to have her grandchildren there, to see them learn to ski there, to show us their two homes.

It had been such a long journey. Arrived at last, we were met at the airport by them both – Richard with his Porsche, Hope in her Mercedes. She was thrilled to see us, but the hint of annoyance for a spilt drop from a juice box on her leather back seat, took me by surprise. The children were very young, eight, six and three.

The next day we were driven to their Whistler place in the mountains to stay together for a week. There was plenty of space – just like their house in Vancouver. The day we got there, Hope insisted I go and have an hour or so skiing with Lorenzo, she would stay with the children with Joel to help. This was the first time she offered to look after them. Perhaps things would be different now we were in *her* home.

I said that I knew their ski school still had to be paid for and that I should stay behind in order to do this. I couldn't pay her back later as I couldn't give her a cheque in Canada. It would be easier if I came with her to pay by card straight away. But she said no, not to worry at all. She insisted. When I returned, I asked for confirmation that she hadn't paid yet, but she replied flippantly in the affirmative – that she had.

"Oh no! How am I going to pay you back? You said you wouldn't do that!"

Her cutting words still ring in my ears - the harsh tone, "Well *somebody* had to pay!"

I didn't understand. I didn't understand what she wanted me to think or see. I felt confused, and I couldn't find any words.

I really wasn't sure what she wanted at all. When Hope had come to stay in *our* home, Lorenzo and I had taken her on trips around Tuscany, out for dinner, or lunch or coffee. We always paid when the bill came – Hope was the guest and she never offered anyway. Richard sometimes offered to pay for our wine he took from our wine shop for the tourists, but his offering was merely a formality – he didn't *expect* to pay.

Here we all were in their home now, and Lorenzo and I were beginning to feel distinctly uncomfortable. Each day got harder, not easier. On the third day there, she announced that she was going out to do the shopping.

"Oh, well do you want me to come with you to help?" I replied eagerly.

"No! I *need* to go by myself!" she replied harshly, her voice void of any diplomacy. Her need to be away from us or perhaps for us to not be there at all was undisguised.

It became clear as time passed that we were more and more an intrusion for them. I was frightened of using anything because she gave the impression that she didn't really want you to use her things. 'Help yourselves' was said but not meant. I had been washing ski socks every day by hand, but by the end of our week's stay I really needed to do a wash in the machine. She hadn't offered and it weighed heavily on me to ask. Then I had to ask how to use it – I didn't want to make a mistake, and then I had to ask to use the dryer.

On another occasion she said, "I can't see a clear line of clean open space on the counter," pointing her arm straight out as if she were giving somebody road directions. "I just can't function with things just put there. Taking up space. It looks messy."

We didn't know where to put ourselves. Lorenzo and I did our best to keep the house tidy, keep the children quiet.

Later in the week, I insisted on coming with her to the supermarket so that I could pay for groceries. Maybe this would make her happy. She seemed pleased when I offered, "Oh well, if you really want to pay." I didn't need to insist.

When it was eventually time for us to leave, Lorenzo and I felt nothing but relief. I daresay there was a relief all round.

CHAPTER TWENTY-SEVEN

That year, 2006, a short time after we came back from our trip to Whistler, there was a good blanket of snow one morning. Even if we'd just been with the snow over in Canada, it's something special when we have it at home. Much to the children's delight, the school closed for a week.

We do try tobogganing down between the rows of vines but it can be quite hazardous. There are stones hidden that can send the toboggan tumbling over and the rows are narrow, giving little space for error – you need to keep straight! There is however always space to make a good snowman. This year, they managed to make two. A snowman and his wife stood side by side looking quite eerie when the light faded. Mr snowman – Brian as we called him, and his wife Brenda, were still there the next morning. And the next. And even when the rest of the snow began to melt, actually within a few days, Brian and Brenda stood there stoically, on the terracotta tiles defying the rising temperature.

We made up stories about Brian and Brenda. How they met and fell in love. I put on a Mr Bean voice for Brian, and we'd invent conversations – how they were feeling about the humans just leaving them there, what those Miceli children didn't know about them - the secrets of snowmen. Anna, our little artist, drew portraits of Brian and Brenda wearing Camilla's blue scarf.

That winter, Hope called regularly and I was polite. I thanked her for our stay, for putting up with us. I supposed others, outsiders, imagined that we were deepening our newfound mother-daughter reunion. I was growing uncomfortable and at odds with her. I felt angry – angry at how she'd been with us in her home – she'd been so inhospitable. Then there were aspects of her character that grated too.

Although she never criticized me personally, I didn't like the way she was so critical of others and particularly of the Akehursts who, by now, I cared about so much. Success in life she measured by career and money; deaf Peter had never made any, so was by her criteria, a failed man. Indeed, he had used '*my* grandfather's money,' she stressed, to bring up his children. (Her grandfather, I must add, was Peter's own father.) It was outrageous, she felt, that anyone could depend on other peoples' money - family money - and not money you earned yourself. And on that score, it was deplorable that her sister Virginia, who had always worked, received financial help from their father.

Hope herself had never worked, never earned a living.

But there was also something wrong in her way with me. Our relationship. On one hand, I knew I should sympathize with her that she had gone through the ordeal of being pregnant in such a difficult time. I *did* sympathize. I knew I should sympathize she had found school so hard. I did. I knew too, that although it wasn't my fault, I should sympathize over the unfortunate circumstance of how she'd got pregnant in the first place. I emphasized my understanding to her. I felt grateful towards her; I felt honoured – honoured that she had accepted me. I was told over and over by so many people – close people – that I was lucky she'd accepted me and lucky that she was who she was – that she wasn't impoverished, needy. She was here for me now wasn't she? So what did I have to complain about?

On the other hand, I couldn't banish the ache. It stayed in the form of a persistent discomfort in both her presence and in her absence. Everything was twisted and I felt misunderstood.

Sometimes I'd meet with the odd person who would have a little more insight into my emotional confusion. A Dutch lady, a guest in one of our apartments, told me how keeping a diary could be so helpful sometimes and bought me a leather bound one herself, and wrote on the inside:

Dear Catriona,

In a book like this, you don't have to follow any rules. You can whisper in it, or bellow out what you wouldn't normally voice, but I would suggest you use a waterproof pen for when you read it in a couple of years!

Hopefully not too lost in translation here is the Dutch poem I told you about:

"My mother has forgotten my name
My child does not yet know what I'm called
How can I feel secure?
Call me, call me, call my name –
Oh call me by my deepest name
It is by you, who I love, that I want to be named"

With love Amelies, over to you.

I followed her advice.

Then the person who set in motion the beginning of some changes – important and very significant changes in my vision of Hope and of me - arrived.

Bernd Strohmaier was a catholic chaplain from Germany and worked in a hospital. He found our agriturismo by chance one year and, with his wife and four children, came to stay for a week. Just as he felt immediately connected to us and the place we had chosen as our home, we too felt connected to him. We developed a comfortable and gentle relationship and he returned many times. He knew about Finn, he knew about Giovanni and after having found Hope, I told him I'd been adopted and the rest of my story. He told me he had heard many a moving story in his life, particularly with the work that he did, but that he had never been quite so moved as he was by mine.

"How is your relationship wiz your mother?" he asked. His English was very good, with that Germanic intonation I've come to recognize so well, from our guests. All his 'th's were said with that letter 'z'.

"Well it's fine. It's very good. I mean she loves me and that's wonderful. I'm just so happy I've found her."

161

"Has she said she was sorry?"

"No. No she hasn't really said that." I replied.

"So how can you say you have a relationship with her, Catriona?" he asked over dinner together in my house.

"I, I don't know. What do you mean?" He'd stumped me.

As he clarified himself, I was suddenly dumbstruck that I had never come to this conclusion myself, that I had not understood. It was so obvious.

"If she has not said sorry," he said, "then you have not begun anything with her. How can you have a beginning if you don't start at the beginning? The sorry is the only beginning. She has to do this for her own peace and for yours." He continued, "Has your grandfather said sorry?"

"No. But he too is ever so happy about me. He has said he's honoured to know me. I'm very grateful."

"But, Catriona, don't you see?" See what? I thought. He went on, "it is *he* that should be grateful to *you*. Not you to him." Your mother too should be grateful to you too. The honour is hers, *not* yours. He too needs to find peace with this, Catriona. He must. He cannot die without putting this in order. Everything has to be in order at the end of our lives. I work with dying people and before they die, they all, without exception, have a need to put their lives in order. In order with their bloodline. He is your direct line. You have come from him through your mother. He has wronged you and he knows that he needs to find his peace and he can only do this with you. You will help him. That is his Truth. There will be, how can I say it in English, like a falling in love when you give him this. Yes, there will be a real love here. This is love. It is all about love. Everyone has their Truth. This is your Truth and you must tell it to him."

"Oh but I can't! It would disturb him so. I have no right! He'd hate me for this. Who am I to be saying this to him? I'm not important enough, I'm just Hope's baby. I was in the way!"

"Catriona, after I have left, you know what I want you to do? You should go and find a special place here at Sugame, I don't think there's a shortage of these kind of places, and you should sit there every day, maybe under a tree, wherever is comfortable for you and tell yourself that you are not guilty. You are not guilty!"

I joined him and Elizabeth his wife for coffee in the garden the next day. It was May. We were sitting under a pine tree when all of a sudden a tiny little bird fell out of its nest and landed on the chair beside us. We all three of us were gripped by the little bird and whether it would make it or not. It was a little stunned but then it just came to, and flew off, its first flight.

"Just like you!" said Bernd and we laughed.

CHAPTER TWENTY-EIGHT

I dreamed I was on a walk with friends. It was late afternoon and we were on our way back from somewhere. It was sunny and warm. I was wearing a t-shirt and shorts. I saw a path leading down to the right and immediately made the decision to take it. It was a shorter but steeper route, and although I didn't know it all that well, I thought it would be fun, and a challenge. You could see that it was a worn path even though it wound through prickly scrub. You'd have to lift your feet quite high in order to avoid being scratched. I felt like a leader, sure, purposeful, and bold and maybe others might follow me. 'But are you sure you know the way?' they asked.

'It's easy.' I boasted while the others took the open, wider, easier and known route.

The path took me steeply downwards into thick woodland. Suddenly it got dark. I couldn't believe how wrongly I'd gauged it, but I was more struck still how quickly the dark had come, not creeping gently as it usually did, but pouncing on me, literally from one moment to the next: I was submerged in pitch black. I held my eyes as wide as they could possibly go in the hope of being able to make out the trees, the scrub and more importantly the path itself. But I couldn't. I put out my arms in front of me walking in a crouched position desperately flailing wildly at the black air in the hope of being able to feel my way instead. My heart was thudding, I was sweating. I was breathing quickly. I was totally lost. I called out but my voice was thin and I knew it could not be heard. Then as quickly as I'd got lost, I found myself at the bottom of this same steep wooded hill, out in the open, and it was broad daylight. My friends were there too and as I looked up at a hostile vertical wall of dense woodland, I wondered how on earth I had managed to get down. But I had.

Now it was time to go back to my therapist, Dott.ssa.

I had never really understood, Dott.ssa Pesci's words on missing maternal love - my birth mother's love - in a child's healthy development: Shelagh had always been my rightful mother and not coming from her genes was irrelevant. Nor had I accepted Dott.ssa Pesci's blunt statement that my birth mother had abandoned me – in my mind she'd done the right thing to give me up. At that time, just after Finn had died, all of this had felt anything but helpful. Nothing would bring Finn back and I had paid little attention.

But since then everything had changed. I had found that missing maternal love. Now I would know the feeling of connection to her. Hope took comfort in any criticism of Shelagh I voiced - I was making it easy for her, wanting her to take up residence in Shelagh's place. I held up her genes like the lost family jewels making Shelagh's imprinting null and void.

We had now returned from the disquieting family trip to Whistler, and I felt no maternal love. Eighteen months of meetings, of conversation, I didn't feel like I was her daughter either. She didn't feel like she was my mother. In addition, the discomfort I had been ignoring since the beginning grew into a very real and tangible pain.

It was right then when Bernd, my chaplain friend, walked into my life.

And Dott.ssa Pesci still there. She had been waiting for me to return.

Now I was ready. Ready to open my eyes. In our renewed conversations I began to give definition to my confusion.

I knew that I'd changed towards Hope. She was no longer a ghost or a fantasy mother. Dott.ssa Pesci made it clear that her giving me away was *not* something righteous and selfless, but the opposite. She had put her life – her happiness – before mine. She had walked away, and never looked back. She had quite literally never thought of me all those years. Now I understood why I felt so angry - that she couldn't feel sorry for this. I couldn't understand how she expected me to just accept it and move on - as if telling me she had never cared, nor thought about me, would not cause me pain.

I discovered too that I could no longer be proud of being adopted. There *wasn't* anything magical. Nor special. And it hurt too to learn that I shouldn't have to feel grateful for it, grateful to be 'chosen'. And what did this famous word 'chosen' mean anyway? To be 'chosen', don't you need to be 'un-chosen' in the first place?

While my understanding was shifting I tried in one way or another to communicate my enlightenment to Hope. But she wouldn't follow me. While she would gladly agree how distorted my image of Shelagh and adoption had been - how her genes were *everything* - she would not feel regret, or pain or guilt. She would not be sorry. "I don't *own* the word sorry," she told me.

I ached with anger. Anger is pain. Perhaps, some might say ignorance really is bliss. Wasn't I better off before all of this? Why suffer pain if you can avoid it by not being aware? Wouldn't it be easier to not know, and to live in the now, not suffer hard truths?

Why love at all if losing hurts so much?

But it's my turn now to say there's no looking back. I will always know that to feel secure, there can be no pretending. Indeed, to feel anything at all - to love – you need the truth. Hope had never loved me. It wasn't my fault. It wasn't my fault she felt no regret for that either. If she couldn't even show it now, then that wasn't my fault either.

Hope still saw herself as the giver and creator of every part of me. All credit to her.

"It moves me so much I want to cry," she had exclaimed to me over a cappuccino in our local village. "That *I* have given you the gift of courage. It has come from *me*. That you have been able to *use* it is so wonderful to watch. You see I have never been able to use my courage."

The comment grated. It was one of those ideas that had newly taken a seat in her mind, I could tell. She'd commented that my strength couldn't possibly have come from Shelagh, insinuating that Shelagh was weak. Now she referred to her own going to England, pregnant with me, doing what she was told, coming back and being able to put it all behind her, as example of the courage that I had so fortuitously inherited from her. I wasn't sure if I was supposed to praise her or thank her, so instead, I agreed with her that it must have been very frightening and commended her for being able to do this. I would like to have asked her if she would have needed more courage still, to break the rules rather than abide by them.

As for my thoughts on the parts Nature and Nurture play in our making, I now know that Shelagh's input has been valid and real. I have come full circle and realized that although she may have had regrets on how she faced her own life, through loving me, reassuring me as she did, she gave me the tools to face up to mine. I'm ashamed that I ever put her down to elevate Hope. For it was Shelagh who read me a bedtime story, or who was there in the middle of the night when I had a nightmare. It was Shelagh who filled up my Christmas stocking, my plate, my bath. It was Shelagh who watched me sing my solo on stage, or listened as I read out loud to one thousand people in the Abbey at school. It was Shelagh who waved me goodbye as I ventured forth on my journey to Italy.

If I have had any courage at all in my life to date, it has certainly not come from Hope as she so claims, but through Shelagh's better channels of love.

CHAPTER TWENTY-NINE

Tears were now streaming down my face as I sat facing her. This was not unusual. I had cried many a time in front of her.

But it wasn't Hope who I faced – I had never cried in front of Hope - but Dott.ssa Pesci.

"But why are you so frightened of her?"

"I don't know!" I sobbed. "She won't want to listen to me. She doesn't want to talk about it. She hates talking about it."

"Well if that's the way she is, let her go back to her precious Canada then!" I looked up from my hands in my lap, to the earnest but calm expression of Dott.ssa Pesci. "What have you got to lose?"

Everything. Nothing.

But I was ready now. Ready to confront her and pack it all in. Be done with her. Finish. Tell her.

"There are some things I need to say to you. Before you go." I heard myself say. I'd left it to the last day of Hope's stay. I'd hated every moment of the days she'd spent with us. So fake - I hadn't been true to myself, let alone to her. Now was my moment. I needed an instruction book to do this.

"So what is it you want to tell me?" She was nice, receptive. I didn't expect it.

I threw myself in, releasing my grip from caution. I said it all. Why couldn't she be sorry? Why hadn't she loved me? How could it be she love me now? I couldn't feel it. How could I feel safe with her? How could I ever feel good enough? Didn't she know it hurt that she left me?

"I *mind!*" I told her. "I *mind* that you never thought about me, had no regrets. You have no regrets now. I mind that you can be so happy, when all I feel is this big black hole in my heart!"

Now my tears were for her and not Dott.ssa Pesci. Tears she had never seen. There was no holding back.

We were in the kitchen of our house. Lorenzo was in the room next door and the children nowhere to be seen. I had my back against the dresser and she was all of a foot away from me. She was crying now, she put her arms tightly around me and held on for life. She buried her head in my shoulder and cried. I mean really cried. Her tears wouldn't stop and the sound that she emitted was like the howl of death.

When they stopped, her hands began to run all over me, stroking my face, cupping my face, caressing my head, my hair, my shoulders. She held my hair at the nape of my neck and with eyes that were soft, she saw me at last.

"I love every part of you. I love every cell in your body. I love this freckle here, and here." She touched my face and put strength in her every word. "Everything. You are perfect. Every which way you are is perfect because it's *you!* I have never loved as I love you. You have no idea. You are everything. You are so *beautiful.* And you're *mine!* You're *my* daughter!"

We stood there facing each other and there was silence. The moment was raw but it was real. I knew that in *that* moment, she loved me.

When Finn and I had had our moment of truth in the corridor of the hospice, I remember going back the next day full of joy. Not joy that he would live, but that we were real now - no stone unturned so that he could go about the task of dying, with me by his side, without the hindrance of falsity. But when I walked in to his room the next morning, it was all gone. He was back under the power of morphine and I shed a tear. He wiped the tear from my cheek with a very cold hand.

169

Hope came into the house the next morning and I was sitting alone at my computer. As soon as I saw her, I had a foreboding feeling, just as I had done when I walked into Finn's room the following day, that there was no continuity from the day before.

She pulled up a chair defiantly and asked me how I was feeling. I told her I felt better than I had in a long time, that I had a sense of a new beginning. It had been good to be able to say what I had for a long time, needed to say. She replied that she on the other hand felt very fragile and raw. She did not feel good at all. I didn't know where all this was going. Hadn't it been a release for her? Didn't she feel good and at peace now? Wasn't it a new beginning for her too? She leaned towards me intently and said, "Do you have any idea what it's been like for me? Do you know that I even tried to commit suicide at one point?" Her bottom lip quivered. I didn't know.

She went on, "I was *enjoying* our time before. I was *enjoying* the honeymoon period. I felt *happy* for the first time in my life! You don't seem to want me to have that pleasure. It was very painful for me yesterday." She continued, "I think you're far more sensitive, emotional than I am. I'm much more cut and dry than you. I can't *be* the mother you want. I can't be perfect. This is me!"

It felt like Hope had managed to annul everything that had been said in the kitchen less than twenty-four hours before. It felt like she didn't want to be sorry after all. If retaliation had not been her intention, then I must have read her wrongly.

After this episode, regret was never shown again, no word about this or the past could be mentioned (she would get prickly and cross if I ever did, and ask me when we would be able to stop talking about this), the sorry was done and dusted. I must be over that *now* for goodness sake. How else would we *move on* in our journey together?

At the time though, I thought the kitchen scene was a turning point, but in essence, the turn never came. I made myself believe in her still because of that scene - like a second chance -

but the truth was that she hadn't changed at all. Her behaviour, her behaviour towards me, was no different.

I should behave like I had always been her daughter. This was impossible – I never *had* been her daughter - and it was for this that I needed to see her want to make up for all the lost years, be *longing* to give. But she made giving look so arduous, it was never automatic, and certainly never a pleasure. Rather it was the opposite. She would present me with a gift, but then hand it to me in such a way that I was never really sure if she really wanted to give it at all, as if she was only doing a duty. Then I had to teach her to think to give the children birthday presents. Then she would use this word, 'expect' - I was never to *expect* anything, like babysit the children for instance, or cook for us like only mothers and grandmothers know how. I thought it should be her pleasure - a pleasure to look after me, care for me, or spoil me a bit - just as it was for Lorenzo's mother or would have been for Shelagh. But it wasn't for Hope. She would be happy doing these things *with* me, but not *for* me.

Of course she was always happy if I were to think of *her* - take her out to dinner, drive her to visit a Tuscan town, or if I should give her something - something precious for her birthday perhaps. And her famous 'moving on' still entailed her need for me to sympathise with her, sympathise for everything that had happened to her, needing me to treat her with thought and care. "With respect," she would say. Only then would she be happy.

For the most part, I didn't feel like doing this for her - pleasing her in the way that I used to. I wasn't ready to be so sympathetic, I wasn't ready to give her the attention she wanted - I still needed that care and attention myself and there was an order to these things for me.

The more I planted myself in the same position, the less she gave. Before, she would always give me something for my birthday either in person or send something in the post. Even then, she'd still manage to complain about the cost of the postage. Now nothing came but a card, and later, when I saw her at my grandfather's, a hand-me-down cardigan of hers that she didn't wear any more. I *think* it was meant to be my belated birthday present. Bought gifts should be deserved.

Another telephone call.

"I was wondering how you were feeling about things between us. I mean is there anything that I do that bothers you?" she had started.

The conversation moved to the subject of that word 'respect' again. She didn't think I respected her.

"Well I don't think you have an awful lot of respect for me either." I dared reply.

Of course this required further explanation. She too thought her behaviour was without fault.

"Well, I find it disrespectful when you slander the British so much." Silence. So I went on to try and explain it to her. "It's like it's a reminder of the original wrong – you know the fact of you leaving me - when you make those disparaging remarks. I think that's why it hurts." I couldn't manage to articulate why her disliking the British in the way that she did was always such a punch in the stomach for me. She habitually made scathing remarks about my country, my people. But why? Did she want me to feel ashamed of them? Be sorry that I was British? Wish that I were Canadian? She was the one who put me there in the first place! I never understood. All I knew was that it grated every time.

At this I heard her voice fill with anger, as she told me how petty I was being. I guess it did sound petty.

"But you can say things against Canadians, and what on earth does it matter, for goodness sake?"

"The difference is that I didn't give you away to Canada!" I tried.

"I was just a girl!" She screamed this one. "I was doing the best thing possible for you going by to England!"

"No you weren't," I went on, "you were doing the best thing for *you*, it was all about you. *You* came first. Not me." My voice was calm, serious, focused. I wasn't shouting like she was.

"I've had ENOUGH of this Catriona. ENOUGH!"

"Well it just hurts," was all I could say.

Then there were only three more words. She hurled them at me with such vehemence, like a bitterly hard slap in my face. "GET OVER IT!" With this, she slammed down the telephone.

I called her the next day, telling myself to be big, and get over it. If I wanted some apology all she could say was how satisfying it had felt to slam the telephone down on me. I told her it was the wrong approach.

"OK, I'm sorry I slammed the phone down." she said flatly, no feeling in the words. Then added, "But it still felt really good!"   and   she   chuckled.

CHAPTER THIRTY

By this time, Camilla was twelve, Tom nine and Anna seven. Hope was ten thousand miles away, so although I would communicate with her, the children had very little contact, or indeed awareness of what was really going on.

When she used to come, they called her Granny-Hope. This had been from the very beginning. They had never even known Shelagh and I had not had time before finding Hope, to put Shelagh in Granny position, albeit absent Granny. So we had decided all of us together that she would be called Granny-Hope. Camilla had been very definite that she should not be just 'Granny'.

Hope was to all intent and purposes, sweet with them. Although, as I say, she never appeared to want to baby-sit, and she was very against spoiling them, she did nothing wrong in their regard either. I *wanted* her to be granny for them. I know she cared about them. I know she felt proud of them, proud to be able to say she was grandmother to them.

As for my children's feelings towards her, I think they just carried my enthusiasm with them, wanting her to be granny because *I* did. In the beginning of our relationship phone calls were long and frequent, nearly always for me and not them, and since there were nine hours times difference between us, our calls were always in the middle of prime family time – five o'clock onwards, just as the children got home from school. So while they were unaware of my discomfort, anger or pain in either her absence or presence, if anything 'Granny-Hope' took Mummy time away from them.

Our three children, Camilla, and Anna all attended the local Italian schools in the village. I speak English to them, and have done since their births. Lorenzo speaks to them in Italian. Children's amazing brains never get it all mixed up - they automatically use the words of one language, and one only, and apply them to the 'correct' parent, and the other language to the other. This happens even when they are just learning to say individual words. 'Acqua' will be used specifically for Daddy, and 'water' for Mummy, 'palla' for Daddy, 'ball' for Mummy, 'cane' – 'dog', 'libro' – 'book', and so on. I find it remarkable.

So while at home they would be switching from one language to another, at school, everything would be very much in Italian. This per se was not a problem – Italian is of course their own language too – but the fact of not speaking it to their mother like the rest of their classmates (there's a reason why we call our primary language 'mother tongue'), would mean, that they each had a smaller vocabulary available to them and less command of Italian.

Italian schooling is rigorous and the vast majority of testing is oral. From third grade onwards, when they add History, Geography and Science to the curriculum (they have all learned to read and write and know their times tables by this time), the teacher will do most of the talking, and the children have to just sit and listen. Listen, listen, listen. They have to go home, open the text book to page such-and-such, read, understand, and say it all back when they go back to school, without looking at the book. They have to just *memorize* it. That's the homework and the oral test is called 'interrogazione' for which they get given a grade. The word itself describes the police-like way in which fear of God is put into them over the whole thing. She will pick on any one child, ask him or her to come to the front, and the child will have to explain all that they have learned from the book with the whole class listening. Just like reciting a poem from memory (they have to do that too).

In history, they start with The Big Bang, then first signs of life on earth, dinosaurs, primitive man, the very early civilizations, followed by the Greeks, Romans and by eighth grade, the will have done the Second World War. Blink and you miss a whole civilization. They pretty much cover everything. It's very systematic. When they go on to secondary school, History goes back to the Greeks, then Romans all over again but in considerably more depth. The method though, remains exactly the same.

On a cultural level, Italian schools are very good. They do know their subjects. They do have a sense of historical time - the past and its influence on the present and the future. They know the great masters of literature, art and science who have come before us and understand how these have influenced the world as we know it today. They all seem to use an expansive vocabulary, and spontaneously too. By 'they', I mean anybody and everybody. Indeed, Italians interviewed on the street, express themselves, I always think, remarkably well. A generalization yes, but a realistic one all the same. It all comes from that very traditional and seemingly old-fashioned schooling they have all been put through.

Thus said, all three of our children had difficulty with this system. My heart would go out to them as they struggled to paraphrase their reading, into nice fluid coherent sentences. Then there was the problem of not always knowing many of the words used. If you miss one word, you can miss the whole meaning of the text. Many words that may come automatically to Italian children, our children had to find a way of memorizing. They were new words. Anna, nine years old, didn't know the word 'lubrificante' (lubricant) when learning about articulation between bones. This was for science. She needed to find a way to remember the word. "Well it begins with the same letter as daddy's name.' I suggested. 'Then you can think of 'loo'! Daddy going to the loo! It finishes with 'cante' like cantare, to sing. Mmm? How's that?" And so she managed to remember that word. Eventually, the whole text would be imprinted in her head, in her own words. She had learned the subject of' l'articulazione'.

A few months after Hope had so defiantly slammed the telephone down on me, I was sitting on the sofa with Camilla, trying to help her read and understand a long text all about how banking in Europe began. It was in fact in the end of the thirteenth, beginning of the fourteenth century. I found it interesting myself: merchants from the relatively new 'bourgeois' society had managed to make considerable amounts of money in their trading. This was because merchant ships from Venice and Genoa were bringing into Italy from the east, spices and pepper - essential for food preservation – woollen cloth, silks, crystal, furs, paper and dyes. All were new products that were very transportable as they took up so little space on board the Venetian or Genovese merchant ships, but more importantly, they were very marketable. The merchants who had made so much money in their trading, decided they could make money by lending it as well. Some even gave up the trading completely, as they soon realized they could earn more money on the interest of lending. Large amounts of money would pass hands even to kings or the pope himself. This was the beginning of banking in Europe. The most important bankers were from Florence and from Lombardy (Milan). In fact in London in The City still today, there is the famous Lombard Street, named after the initial bankers from that region in Italy.

I was trying to explain to Camilla what lending money was all about.

"Let's say you want to buy an iPhone?" I began. "Well you don't have enough money do you?"

"No."

"Well, what you could do is borrow the money. Then bit by bit, you can pay it back."

"Really? Can I have an iPhone then?"

"Camilla this is just hypothetical."

"What's hypothetical?"

"It means we're just supposing, ok? I'm not getting you an i-Phone! Now, the thing is, the person who lends you the money, doesn't just lend. He wants something out of lending to you. So he says, 'well you have to pay me 3% interest each month.' That means that each time you pay back say €50, You have to pay back € 51.50 instead - just a little extra which you don't really notice. That's his 3 %. So after twelve months, well he's earned, let me see, €1.50 x 12 is € 18. That's what he gets from lending you the money. You see? And if he did that for a hundred people, well that would be um, € 1800, right? Just from lending money."

"Mm huh. I get it."

It was three o'clock in the afternoon and I had her full attention and we were just getting into it, sitting snugly together. I was also enjoying time with her by herself – without the other two younger ones around because they were still at school. Camilla now in 'scuola media' would finish school at lunch time. The other two, in 'scuola primaria' would spend the whole day and have lunch at school. I've always found it special helping any one of them with their school work, and find myself involved and committed. I can't bear the idea of their self esteem in school being reduced to dust just because of such a rigorous educational system.

This was the setting when the telephone rang. I knew it was her. Hope. I hadn't called her for a while - had less and less desire to speak with her - ever since her screaming at me to *get over it!* I could feel her sitting out the wait in the hope that I would succumb, and call her. I hadn't.

"No Mummy! Please! Please don't answer it." begged Camilla.

I didn't want to but felt if I didn't, I'd make things even worse. I felt obliged to answer.

It was an angry call. She had clearly built up enough anger to give herself the courage to call and hurl her resentment at me. It was only six in the morning for her. She must have been thinking of nothing else and had woken with a mission to accomplish.

"So what's the matter then?" Were her first very undisguised angry words.

"What do you mean? Nothing! I'm fine." But I knew she had detected that all was not well. It wasn't. I didn't want to carry on a relationship with her. I was done. If anything was going to exist between us, it could only be superficial.   "I am losing sleep because of you, I am aging because of you," She started, stressing the word 'sleep' and 'aging'. She complained that I didn't call her, that I didn't take any interest in her.

"You never ask me how I am! I mean I could be sick and you wouldn't even know! I feel like I'm the one doing all the work in this relationship."

And then she complained that I didn't respect her. I didn't seem to need her. She backed herself up by saying that Joel and Konner too felt that I didn't love them any more. I told her that they could tell me themselves, but they could start on their part by perhaps remembering my birthday.

Then I tried to soften it all by mentioning my relationship with Shelagh saying that friction could be normal between mother and daughter.

She replied with sympathy. Not for me, but for Shelagh.

"It must have been very hard for her to bring up a daughter like you."

She finished by accusing me of not loving her any more.

I wrote to her after this conversation. I told her I didn't accept what she had said. I told her she could call any time she wanted but that I didn't feel ready to call her.

She never did. I have not heard her voice since.

PART THREE

CHAPTER THIRTY-ONE

I need to turn the clock back now to 2008. This would be two years before that brutal and final conversation with Hope. I was sitting at my kitchen table with both her and her sister, my aunt Virginia.

"I don't think she read it," said Virginia.

"I think she did," said Hope.

"Well would you read it?" Virginia turned to me.

"Me? No, I don't think so." I answered. "I guess I'd phone him and ask him if he'd want me to open it for him."

"Yes but don't forget her husband was thousands of miles away, and also away for a long time and she probably didn't know exactly when she was next going to see him, and there she is completely alone, with two letters in her hand, handwritten - same handwriting, same woman, both recorded delivery. I know I'd be dying to open them!" Hope exclaimed. "I mean your mind would be racing wouldn't it? Yes I definitely think she read it."

"Mmm. I don't know. I wouldn't open it either. I'd have to give it to him, or at least tell him on the phone, and ask if he'd like me to open it and tell him what it was all about." mused Virginia. "Then I'd find out wouldn't I?"

"Ok, so, let's say she didn't open it. Then why did she take two months to pass it on to him?" I said. "Don't forget he only found out about the letter the moment she gave it to him in person over two months later."

"Cos she read it already!" said Hope. "I told you!"

"Well she should have been relieved then!" interjected Virginia, "relieved that he wasn't having an affair!"

"Well she can't have been all that relieved otherwise she wouldn't have kept it secret from him."

"Why didn't she want to tell him though?" I questioned.

But we didn't know the answer to that. If she had read it, there was no explanation why she didn't tell her husband that he had a daughter - me - a daughter he never knew he had.

There we were the three of us, having a light-hearted bet over whether my birth father's wife had or had not read my letter. I looked at one, then the other as I sat between them.

Hope and Virginia were both staying with me. So different from her sister, Virginia is all 'mother' - kind, bossy, and fiercely protective of her own brood.

"Now Catriona, does Tom have a hammer?" she'd asked me over the phone before coming.

"A hammer? No! There are tons of hammers around here!"

"You mean he doesn't have one of his own? All boys have to have their own hammer!"

So when she came, amongst a huge assortment of gifts, she brought him his own hammer and made sure he wrote his name on with an indelible pen.

When Hope came to meet me for the first time back in 2004, I began to shape my understanding of my father being a real person – flesh and blood. Unlike the image I had created of her for as long as I could remember, I had never created any image of my birth father. Throughout my life, he had been, to all intents and purposes, a nonentity, as if I had magically been brought into existence through her body - hers alone. I knew rationally that he was a part of my DNA - I might well have inherited parts from him too - but he was never the figure of 'father', as she was 'mother'. I wonder sometimes if people conceived by sperm donors, might feel the same.

But in that time when I first knew Hope, I was more than curious to see a picture of him. I wrote to McGill University in Montreal and they sent me back a black and white photograph from 1964. There were two others in the picture with him, and no indicator as to who was who. But to me, there was no doubt. The one in the middle could be none other than my father. He looked so familiar. I recognized instantly the shape of his head, the shape of his half smile, the small scale of him beside the other two. He was wearing glasses which I need too. It felt good. It felt strange.

"He's on his *third* marriage," Hope had said with disdain. "Nancy's brother asked around and he's been described as a disgruntled sixty two year old!"

And the latest, in 2006, he'd moved to Arizona. Each time I listened, she had no idea of the impact her words were having upon me. She couldn't know what the realization process felt like. Learning details about an ordinary or banal event from the past – something she could remember – was like discovering secrets, and one by one, they were being handed to me like jewels.

"I can't remember ever seeing him again back then, but once I did see him in a game – hockey perhaps – and I noticed him throwing out these things to us the spectators - leaflets or something - before the game had started," and as she spoke, she gesticulated his movement. Instantly a moving picture like a mini clip of a film, took shape in my mind: a tall good-looking young man, dressed in sports gear, tossing and walking, tossing and walking, in a straight purposeful line, brisk, confident, carefree.

She told me that his mother had had blue eyes. "You didn't tell me!" I exclaimed.

Step by step, detail by detail, I was absorbing a new reality: I *had* a father, and that this one was *mine*. I could be like everybody else. Here I was thinking about him, and all the while, he would be totally oblivious to my thoughts, just going about his business in some other part of the globe.

Hope wrote to him in September 2006, to tell him he had a daughter. I'll never forget it. Not his response, but the fact of Hope just telling him. I held the phone to my ear looking out at

183

the vineyards from my bedroom window. She had finally realized, she told me, that this was the right thing to do. I was amazed. I never thought she would. I thanked her. I told her she was brave. Above all, I respected her. She had done it for me. She received a signature from his office that the letter had been received.

"Now he knows about you Catriona," she said. "At least he knows he has a daughter. What he does with this information is yet to be revealed. But remember he knows."

I felt honoured that my father knew about me. What would he be thinking? Had he looked at my picture on my web site Hope had indicated to him? All of a sudden, I was no longer the examiner surreptitiously viewing him through a telescope, but the examined, awaiting his judgement.

But no judgement came. I waited with trepidation those first few days. Then it was a week. How strange to hear nothing. He did have the letter – we knew that. Weeks passed into months. Then it was already a year.

There was only one conclusion. He didn't want to know. I was surprised, but not shocked, disappointed but not hurt, but most of all, I was dissatisfied. It was unfinished business and there was nothing I could do about it. There was nothing I could do to make his 'no' into a 'yes'.

As time passed, I questioned the facts. Had he really received Hope's letter? If he hadn't (the letter had only been signed for by someone in the office), then there wasn't proof *beyond reasonable doubt*, that he really didn't want to know me.

There was only one way to find out. I should write a letter myself, by hand, and send it recorded delivery to his home address, not the office, with a request for the signature of its receiver. Him. This way, I could at least be sure that the letter had reached his hand, and his hand only. I just had to be sure he *really* didn't want to know me.

January 2008 I finally plucked up the courage. It would be my last shot.

Standing at the post office, letter in hand, I was trembling. With this letter, also went also my hope: as long as there was doubt, there was still space for hope. If there was still no reply, there was nothing left to hold onto at all.

As I stood there in the queue, I looked at the various people before and after me. Bored, impatient. A young mother with a pram and a baby, a man dressed as builder definitely in a hurry, an ancient couple one more hunched than the other. These were people paying their bills, collecting their pension, posting a parcel. All of them oblivious to my story.

Finally came my turn. The letter was out of my hands.

About ten days later, I received an orange coloured postal receipt. I could barely believe my eyes when I realized exactly what it was: *his* signature. There it was - his name written by his very hand in the signature box. He *had* the letter. At last. No more doubt. I held onto this orange paper – this very paper he had touched and looked at - like it was a lottery ticket and I had won.

Now at last, I would hear from him. I expect he would write a letter like mine – you don't reply by email to a letter like this. I'd watch out for it of course. How long? Perhaps a couple of weeks? How long would he take?

However, when I examined the signature on the orange return slip more closely, I realized it was not exactly *his* signature. It read, 'Fiona Cawthorn', not 'Fraser Cawthorn'. It was his wife's signature.

In fact I didn't hear from him. Not then, nor the next month, nor the next, nor the next.

Now I knew for sure that he *really* didn't want to know me. Obviously his wife had passed him the letter, he'd read it, but for some reason, he didn't want to reply. Easier not to. I accepted at long last.

Then, three months later, an email suddenly appeared in my inbox. Fraser Cawthorn was the sender. I was too astonished to take it in. I stared at the black lettered name. Fraser Cawthorn's name was in my inbox.

I clicked to open it.

He began: *'Catriona, I am sitting here in my apartment in Tokyo re-reading your letter, which my wife brought* me last week. I would have responded when I first received it, but chose to wait a few days to gather my thoughts. I am sorry that this is an e-mail but you will get this message a whole lot sooner......

And on he wrote in this gentle fashion: '..Now I just want to communicate my feelings to you and, out of respect, communicate with you.......

.... I am not upset or concerned in any way over the suggestion that I am your father. I think I understand your anxiety you have over not knowing your father and the feeling of something unfinished, which comes out loud and clear in your letter. It was indeed written very well. I do not find it threatening in the least'

But loud and clear in *his* communication, there was one factor that I had never considered. Why had it not occurred to me?

He might not believe that he could be my father.

He didn't.

Yes, he had received Hope's letter but had found it hard to believe, so had chosen to ignore it.   Oddly, his letter went on to give details of his life, his two daughters Vicky and Stephanie, his nine-month assignment in Japan, his forthcoming retirement. Huge photographs were attached, both of himself with his wife Fiona, and himself with his two daughters.

He finished with: '*I am not sure how to end this note. I have no qualms about further communication. I can hear you calling out in your letter...*

And at the bottom, he left his telephone and fax numbers there in Tokyo.

CHAPTER THIRTY-TWO

Very quickly, the bets that had gone on around my kitchen table felt long gone. One week later while Hope and Virginia were still staying with me, I was speaking with him on the telephone. I, in a farm in Tuscany, he, in the centre of Tokyo. I sat quite calmly as I listened to his voice. I was wondering what on earth he could be thinking. Thinking of me. A replay of the telephone scene when I first spoke to Hope.

Hope had been right. His wife, Fiona, had in fact opened and read my letter he told me, but never mentioned it to him in the time she had kept it.

"Really? Oh so she gave it to you when she came to visit then?"

"Yes, but funnily enough, not until after she left. Well, I mean, she handed me the envelope, opened, just as she was leaving for the airport." He said it as if he were telling a story. It *was* a story. A real story. I hung on to every word. "So I said, 'what's this?' and she just said, 'well, just take a look. I think you'll find it interesting.'"

Surreal as my first conversation with Hope, so was this, as we chatted about ourselves. I told him I knew it was hard to believe that Hope could have got pregnant like that, but without going into detail, it was possible. He said we would have to do a DNA.

I didn't like him not believing it.

"Yes, of course." I agreed.

187

Then we were coming to a close. I could feel it. I could feel the ideas of what to say, running out. And yet I still was no closer to knowing what he felt. I had to know. Suddenly aware there was really nothing to lose, I plucked up the courage to ask.

"So can I ask you what you are feeling right now – what you are feeling about all of this?"

"I'm thinking," he replied, so slowly that I could feel him choosing each word with precision, plucking them one by one from his mental dictionary, "that after this brief conversation, I'd like to discover that the DNA proves me to be your father."

Excitement fluttered in my belly, these few words speaking unbelievable volumes. They gave me that same sense of honour that I had when I first spoke to Hope: he would like to recognize me.

All of a sudden, only three days later, to my total surprise, a DNA kit from a London laboratory arrived.

I thought it would be something more complicated. I imagined DNA testing to be carried out in a laboratory with sterile syringes and phials. The simplicity and homey nature of the kit took me by surprise. There were just three sticks just like cotton buds for cleaning your ears in a sealed plastic bag. There were instructions – very simple ones – telling the user to just rub the bud on the inside of the cheek, to then put it in the designated envelope, seal it and send back to the laboratory in London where it had come from. There was a code handwritten on the envelope. In just seven working days, I would have the answer.

I did as required and sent it off the next morning.

With this, Fraser - my unproven birth father - and I immediately started to develop a rapport. I was writing to mention the kit, he was writing back, and on we went comparing notes, not just of the facts of it, but of what we were feeling. It is the most peculiar limbic state to be in – being kept on hold to find out if this is your real father – if this is your real daughter. We were two total strangers to one another, and yet we were sharing such an extraordinary common ground – a place where no one else could be. No one but us.

By this time, I couldn't bear the thought that the results could prove negative. One could not be sure, just as you can't be sure you've passed an exam, even when you know you did well. Nothing is certain until you are given the proof.

By now I didn't want anyone else to be my father.

He too, was so keen to be my father. Perhaps he already liked me and decided it would be exciting to have a new daughter. We were *both* excited. He wrote, *'I would like you to know that I will still be there for you if in the unlikely event, the test proved me not to be your father.'*

I lapped it up, despite the non-sense of this, pleased with such support.

On May 15th 2008, I received an e-mail from 'DNA Bioscience' with a copy of the result attached. I had Lorenzo open it for me to tell me the result.

'The probability of paternity of the alleged father is 99.9997%'. My ever-patient husband smiled for me and opening his arms wide, enfolded me into his safe body.

The day after the DNA results arrived, Fraser wrote: *'As I was listening to my iPod, this came up and I immediately said to myself this is how I feel right now when I think of you and me, so I had to tell you. That feeling of a 'connection' between us doesn't do it justice, it's more than that.'*

No one has ever sent me a piece of music to express their feelings for me. It was the most romantic thing. The music was called, 'Bilits' by Sarah Brightman. I knew the song as soon as I saw the title. It had been an LP we used to listen to at school. The album cover had been of naked young women, sprawling themselves over branches of a tree. I put my earplugs in and listened. This version that he was sending me was lush, was soft, extremely sensuous.

Yes, I recognized the fact that the music expressed feelings that weren't quite right, but I was intent on my journey with my new father, and he was here, and he was thinking about me, and nothing else mattered. He had feelings for me and this was wonderful. If he felt this connected with me, his daughter, then I knew that his words of reassurance—'*this one is for keeps*' were true.

My new father and I began communicating quite furiously, and in such a way, that very quickly, we were a part of each other's lives. He was there living alone in Tokyo and I was carrying on with my everyday life with my family, the tourists and the farm here in Tuscany. Soon we would both expect an email from each other just about every day.

Everything I did or said pleased him; I could do no wrong. I inspired feelings in him he had never had before, he told me, "*I am gradually unfolding myself to you, but that is only because you, Catriona, enable it in me. I think I might have said once that you wear your heart on your sleeve for the whole world to see. My heart is buried deep down. The truly beautiful thing about us is that you have brought it to the surface, slowly but surely, and just by being yourself. I feel totally comfortable in your presence. I know that you will handle it with care, as I do with yours, and the returns on this little bit of risk are enormous. I feel blessed that I have found you, and I wasn't even the one doing the looking. You have brought out the very best in me, and if that makes you feel pride in yourself, pride which translates into a feeling of belonging, then I have to give you all the credit.*"

He then used the analogy of a ship roaming the seas but that finally it had come home to port. I was the ship. It was magical, dreamlike, to believe I had come home. I was Cinderella.

By the time he wrote to me about his heart, he had already won mine. One letter tumbled into another and everything he said, or I said, fuelled the excitement. In a letter where he began defining himself to me, he spoke too of my voice:

"*I am your biological father but I am also your, not sure how to express the right word - your guardian, your kindred spirit, your devotee, your friend? This friend is forever. I promise···.*

······. *You have that speaking voice, then you have the soft loving voice when you are speaking to me with your heart open.*

Yesterday was the first time I had actually heard it. Yes I am talking about the sound waves. It was different, very soft and very loving. That was the voice I so dearly want to hear again and I am kicking myself for not engaging you at that level so it could carry on."

Before I knew it, I was impossibly and intricately entangled with him and he with me. There was no retreat.

Thursday 12th June 2008

I dreamed last night that I was going to meet Fraser. I was going to his house. He'd insisted. I was with my mother Shelagh in the car. I glanced at her – her appearance mattered. I was driving my white Fiat Panda; all of a sudden, Fiona, Fraser's wife, pulled out from behind me in her pink car. She didn't see me. I followed her to find Fraser's house. When I got there, I drove up next to her, got out of my car and rushed up to her to greet her but she ignored me totally.

Then I was running, running quite frantically, along a paved path which would lead to his house. I looked at my watch to see how long this journey would take – from the beginning of the path to his house – to the future. Like a sort of countdown to my new life. I passed some people who were from my past, I knew this because they had the Wiltshire country accent of where I grew up. Then I passed a lady who was clutching a baby. The baby was her grandchild and she was holding him so lovingly, cherishing him tightly, and looking up to the sky as if in praise, like he was a miracle baby. There was an immense sense of gratitude and an even greater sense of love for this baby - this baby was special.

I arrived in the middle of a village, the village where my first boarding school was when I was eight. I so wanted to get to Fraser's house. Then I arrived but instead of walking down the steps that lead to the basement, I leapt over the wall, such was my sense of urgency – I had to get there. I rang the bell. The doors were automatic and opened before me. There was a throng of people. I stripped off my coat to be ready for him. To my right was the staircase and as I looked up, coming down quite gracefully, was a drop-dead-gorgeous looking young man with dark hair. He was in his early twenties. This was Fraser, nothing like the man in the actual picture I have of him in his twenties – he was film-star good looking, but it was definitely him and no other. He was at the bottom of the stairs now and looked at me up and down. I ran into his arms, jumping up wanting him to pick me right up like a child, but he couldn't hold me up and he dropped me and we tumbled down together at the bottom of the stairs in a heap. He was above me, his face so close to mine, his eyes – I was melting into them because they were my eyes, and his face was just centimetres away. My heart was pounding as we held each other's stare. It was pounding so hard that it woke me up and it took a while, in my awakened state for it to calm down.

I told Lorenzo about these feelings for my father. I shared everything I could. I talked about him constantly, with anybody who cared to listen.

I had found my identity – I was so like him, thought like him, felt like him. He was intelligent and now he was my knight in shining armour. He would always be there for me, from now 'until death do us part'. I should never have to worry, he told me.

Lorenzo sat by patiently. He never tried to halt me or suggest that I may have set my expectations unrealistically high. Sometimes he got fed up and would let me know, but he also enjoyed the happiness that I was projecting. It was for all to see and there were benefits in that.

Besides, Fraser was in actual fact physically ten thousand miles away in Japan. I had not even met him.

"I've had three woman in my life," he explained. "Now four. Each time, it has got closer to the right one. First there was Jill, then a little better with Kathy, then I thought I'd found everything when I met Fiona. And now this! I've found *you*."

I felt proud of myself for being 'The One' - the best one on his ladder of women.

"We both know that this is not a father-daughter thing. It's a man-woman one. Well put it this way, if you'd been born a boy, I wouldn't feel this way about you." He said as I sat on the sofa one afternoon. I can still feel the disillusionment that swept over me as his words reached me. I froze.

"No, that's not true. This is a father-daughter thing. Not because you are a man! I already have a man!"

But he did not hear these words. These were the words held back in fear, that could not reach my lips – they did not come out. They remained in the safety of my head. No damage could be done - I would lose him if I didn't agree – and silence was my only reply.

One night some time on from this episode, late, I was listening to his loving words clutching the telephone to my ear. All of a sudden, I felt a strong tingle, creep all over my skin. It was the strangest feeling, a wonderful feeling, and one that my mother, Hope, had talked about herself, but which I had never understood. Just after our first phone call – Hope and I that is - she told me how she had stood in front of the mirror having got out of the shower, and, looking at her own naked body, felt her skin tingle from top to toe. In looking at herself, the dramatic realization that I had come from her, was so compelling, that it provoked an extraordinary sensation on her skin, as if every part of her was tingling – buzzing – with life.

In this moment while listening to my father, I understood what she had meant. The realization that he was a part of me or rather I a part of him, was like an explosive understanding, and I immediately told him, and described the physical sensation that I was experiencing. It wasn't sexual I stressed, but just new, nice.

"Do you feel me now as a man or a father? He asked.

"A father," but these words again remained locked inside me, "a man," I said, and knew my own falsity.

"That's the first time I've heard you say that," he replied, his tone full of congratulation. I had 'got there' too now. This was where he wanted me to be.

The weeks went by. We would meet at the end of the summer, we hoped. The relationship carried on in this extraordinary vein. It was very intense and took up so much of my time and space.

Children always sense when things are not right, and have their own way of telling you. Sadly we adults are often good at conveniently misinterpreting their messages, but there was one occasion that I didn't miss. I came into the house one afternoon to find my five year old daughter, Anna, with glue all over her hands and several of the letters of the keyboard of my computer strewn all over the table. There were gaping holes in the keyboard, filled with glue as she was anxiously trying to rectify the damage she had done, by sticking the letters back. I was horrified, first at the sight of my computer, but then my alarm turned very quickly to her. It broke my heart to see her feeling so guilty over what in essence was my fault. It came to me in such a flash, my neglect so obvious.

"Anna, were you feeling angry at the computer because Mummy prefers it to you? Does it take me away from you?" I asked her as I tucked her up that night.

"Yes." Came her simple and honest reply.

I made no excuses, no justifications. I said sorry, plain and simple. I was sorry that I'd hurt her by spending so much time with the computer, but I was glad that she let me know. I told her that she wouldn't need to hurt the computer again, and that I'd mend it. We'd spend some special time together the next day. I *was* on my computer an unreasonable amount of time and far too involved with a person that meant nothing whatsoever to the rest of my family. That could come all in good time when they would be able to meet him. He was their grandfather and would feel it too, one day.

Still, while I could contain my behaviour, the feelings didn't change.

"But Catriona, you must understand you have not even met your father!" Dott.ssa Pesci tried explaining to me. "You can't really know him until you have."

But the virtual reality felt real. I *did* know him. Dott.ssa Pesci wasn't God after all. I knew him so well. I knew him as well as I knew my right hand. He was a part of me and I of him and I had found the person that I had been needing to find – the person who understood my whole being and the way I ticked. Because he was my father.

194

Furthermore he had the perfect wife. What more could I ask for? He talked of Fiona a lot, and very much wanted me to telephone her and make a connection with her. I was so *like* her in every way, he insisted. She was the most sensitive, intelligent, kind and sympathetic person, a true 'giver', compassionate and understanding. Everybody in his family loved her, they had all warmed to her so, and she was wonderful with Stephie's boys (his elder daughter, Stephanie, had three boys, the younger Vicky, one little girl). That was Fiona. Thanks to her, his relationship with the girls had improved and they were speaking with him now. Fiona and my father would carry me, I would be enfolded by her into the bosom of their rock solid relationship where I would be safe and loved by them both. I had nothing to worry about.

The woman of his dreams who fixed everything, even though he had waited fifty-two years and gone through two other marriages to find it, but he was happy now. What safer place was there, to be able to work through the ups and downs and complications of a father-daughter adoption reunion?

"Fiona and I probably email, telephone or message one another just about everyday," he told me out of the blue.

A wave of fear washed through me. Why then hadn't she mentioned my letter? He had even gone all the way back to the US for a wedding, spent the weekend with her. Yet she kept the letter from him.

Uncertainty about Fiona grew into a silent discomfort which I kept from him.

But then one day he brought up the issue himself. Out of the blue, he told me that Fiona behaved oddly sometimes. Once she'd been caught for 'drunk driving' but she had never told him. He found out through a different channel. He openly began mulling over with me why she'd not told him about my letter but was unable to come up with an answer. He said that he would ask her gently when she came to stay with him there in Tokyo. She might not want to talk about it.

After her visit, he called me. It was all perfectly simple: Fiona wasn't like me, and I shouldn't expect her to be. He was almost cutting in his tone. He had changed. What was going on? She didn't think like him either, and hadn't picked up on any of the things in my letter that he had. She hadn't thought my letter significant, or seen any urgency. She had put it away and forgotten about it. She was an extremely busy person, had other things on her mind, I must understand, and I couldn't expect her to give my letter the priority I thought that it deserved. She viewed life more simply, never making things complicated in her head.

Even if this explanation sounded strange, I should accept it as her truth. She was a complete stranger to me after all. Perhaps my hand-written letter, pleading to be acknowledged was too naked, too needy. Perhaps she was frightened by my so evident need to be in his life.

Dear Fraser,

I would like to know you!!

Whatever I say and however I even start this, it sounds wrong. So in asking myself, 'what is it exactly you want to say?' the answer is just that: I would like to know you. It's that simple.

Over a year ago, you received a letter all about me, my existence, from Hope Richardson. She is my birth mother. She became pregnant by you 43 years ago. (As I understand it, this would be hard to believe given the circumstances of that conception, but apparently true. There was no one else but you that once, and I was the result.) She went to England, gave birth there, and gave me up for adoption. You never knew. I found her 3½ years ago after all my adoptive family had died.

I've been trying hard to believe your silence is due to your never receiving her letter, but if that's the case, well, it's well and good that I'm now writing, and if that's not the case, then your silence prompts me to try and reach you again.

I can't imagine what it must be like for you to have this information thrown at you and then to be expected to not only believe it but to have to do something about it. 'What on earth am I supposed to do?' maybe you're thinking. I simply can't know what it's like for you and I cannot possibly know why you don't respond. What I can know however, is what it's like for me.

Not being recognized by one's birth family, be it mother or father, hurts. It leaves such a huge open space in one's life – the not knowing. It does matter where we come from, otherwise thousnadss of adopted or orphaned people wouldn't ever have any interest in finding their roots. Without roots, there's a feeling of floating and not being tied to anybody or anything from the past. We just sort of arrived on the planet somehow. Adoptive parents can give a fair amount but they can't give you this – your history and real sense of belonging in the world. We need these genetic markers, the mirror image, to tell us who we are. But we adoptees must somehow invent that mirror image taking it from our adoptive parents and their families; but we know deep down that they and their forefathers have nothing to do with us at all, but that out there somewhere, the real mirror does exist.

We hear stories all the time about people being re-united and we are moved by these stories, and out of the thousands of those, this one is yet another: Hope and I are re-united. I am connected to her and her family in the one way I have yearned for all of my life. I have my 'genetic mirror' at last. But only one half. It's time I found that other one. Please don't under-estimate the importance of this just because I have found my mother.

Lastly, once you believe this, perhaps you too could gain something from this: I'm a daughter you never knew you had – does that have to be a burden or can it be a gift? There aren't even any strings attached: I'm not claiming the daughter position. How could I possibly? How could you possibly all of a sudden become 'my father'? It's out of the question. I ask nothing but to know you. Furthermore, I'm lucky enough to have a privileged life, living in a beautiful place; I'm safe and well, supported by a wonderful husband and 3 wonderful children, my mother and all of her family......this is not a cry for some material gain. I beg you to consider all this. Knowing that you're there but not knowing you, is even quite haunting and it would be not only a pleasure, but a relief to hear from you. As total strangers to one another, perhaps nothing will come of it, but at least we will not have allowed room for regret. Life is short......

A few pictures – with all best wishes,

Catriona Miceli (pronounced Catrina – gaelic spelling!)

CHAPTER THIRTY-THREE

"Fiona and I started by having an affair together," my father told me on the telephone. "I was living in New York during the week and going back to my second wife Kathy in Toronto, at the weekends. Fiona too was married to someone else. Actually we were both on our second marriages. It was when we allowed ourselves to be honest with our feelings that we realized we had to leave our respective spouses and be together permanently."

He explained to me that in the long run, although many people got hurt at the time, everyone was better off for their decision. He had been honest and brave. Everyone benefitted by being able to see Fraser so happy. His daughters from his first marriage were better off for this reason, and he was even now on speaking terms with their mother, Jill, after so much silence and hatred. It was through Fiona that he had learned to love himself and in doing that, he said, he was able to love others.

He proudly went on to tell me of the extraordinary way in which Fiona left her husband, quite literally slipping out the back door. She couldn't tell her husband she was leaving him, he had no idea, and so she waited until he had gone to work, called in a removal van to take away all the furniture, just leaving a note for him that he wouldn't be seeing her again, and in this way, she was gone from their marriage for ever. He had no idea, Fraser told me. What a frightening husband Fiona must have had if she'd had to leave him in that way I thought!

My father on the other hand, had felt the need to give more explanation to Kathy, his wife. She had been very upset and never got over their marriage ending after fifteen years. He had after all brought up Kathy's two children as well, and they had been a family. He never spoke with or saw them ever again.

Then it became obvious that something was out of place with his own children, Stephie and Vicky. He told me this himself. They were not close to him at all. He went on to tell me all about their mother Jill, his first wife, and the disastrous relationship he'd had with her. He had put up with her for *ten* years, he stressed, and then told me that the '*sex was totally unsatisfactory*'. He went on to say that as things got really bad with her, she would exasperate him so much that once he had struck her, which he wasn't very proud of but she had pushed him to his limits - it really had been her own fault. Then when he was eventually leaving her for good, she didn't believe that he would actually go. He'd started having affairs with other women after the first couple of years but remained married to Jill all the while. He nearly left her when he had his first affair, after Stephanie was born, but before Vicky. She had begged him to stay, and so he had, hence the age gap between the two girls. Just before he was really leaving her for good though, and before he'd sorted out a place to live for himself, he had with her, '*the best sex ever for two weeks solid*'. He stressed the word 'ever'. And then he left. He finished the story by saying that it was because she was, '*only trying to please him*', so desperate she was to have him stay.

I was sitting in our armchair in the kitchen in one of our long telephone calls that summer, and not wanting to have any negative thoughts of him, I made no judgement. I simply absorbed all the information on the history of his marriages.

The summer passed by. Before I knew it, October had come round again.

It was a Saturday, the sun was shining and we were outside. There were six children – our three, and three cousins. All were bare feet, shorts or trousers rolled up, standing in a circle, totally absorbed by something. But I couldn't see what. It was evidently very funny for the sounds they were all making.

On closer inspection, I saw that there was a big plastic bowl on the ground, and they were taking it in turns to stand in it, stump around a bit, squeal in delighted disgust, get out and let another have a turn. The bowl was half full of something. Squelch squelch as they stood in it.

Grapes. Freshly picked Sangiovese grapes. "Mummy we're making grape juice!" Anna couldn't help laughing. Purple feet. I couldn't help but laugh back. What a picture.

They were freshly picked because we were in the middle of *La Vendemmia*. It was lunch time. There were people milling around, hungry, having been picking grapes all morning in the vineyard. They would eat the food I had prepared, set out on garden tables in the 'piazza', the centre-piece of our farm. While waiting, the children were still busy with their juice. They managed to find a sieve, bowls, a funnel, and empty bottles of all shapes and sizes. They filled the bottles with the juice and put them 'on sale' set out with price tags, cups, the works. All six children stood behind the table waiting eagerly for customers. Passer-byers - guests from apartments, or friends and family helping with harvest – came to their 'shop' to investigate, and not having witnessed the not so hygienic methods of extracting the juice, bought a cup or two.

"Excuse me, would you like to buy a cup of grape juice?" Camilla all sweet and polite.

"Well, how much are you selling it for?" A friendly Canadian man rubbed his hands together ready for the game with them.

"Questi sono i prezzi! Cinquanta centesimi per un bicchiere." The almost defiant answer coming from Olivia.

"One cup is fifty cents. Two cups one euro. But if you buy three cups, it's only one euro and twenty-five," came Tom's eager clarification.

"Well I'll have two then please." A sip. "Mmmmmm! It's delicious!" he exclaimed, stressing the whole word. It delighted the children, eyes all bright, more laughter.

The *vendemmia*. That dreaded and beloved time of year for harvesting the grapes. I say dreaded because it's a tense moment. Lorenzo's hard work, a whole year's work, is all funnelled in to just three days. Three very vital and exactly chosen, days. Once the grapes are picked, there's no more to worry about – they can't change now – no more ripening, or moulding. The dye is cast and the wine will be what it will be. Different every year. Now it can rain, it can shine, it can hail, it can do whatever it wants. We don't care anymore. Our grapes are safely in. But those days of picking are crucial.

There's a hum of busyness during the harvest time. Workers are family and friends. We're a team. I love being down there in the vineyard, secateurs in hand, where we pick and chat and joke. Lorenzo is the big boss. We take his orders.

"*Solo la parte in alto di questi filari. Non la parte in giù. Non il Cabernet. Il Sangiovese va da qui in giù fino a là. Va bene? Ho messo sacchetti per indicare fin dove.*"

"Only the top part on these rows. Not those ones down there – not the Cabernet. The Sangiovese goes from here down to the middle of these rows, Ok? I've put plastic bags on top of the poles to indicate the spot where you stop picking. Only Sangiovese today."

His marking method is terrible! We never understand where we are supposed to stop. Then when he is explaining to the fifteen or twenty of us, we are usually always so spread out in the rows, hidden by foliage that not everyone can hear. So relays of shouted out messages go across the rows. Then there's always still a little handful of pickers who haven't got it.

"No, not there. You've gone too far. Don't pick there! You have to move over a row and go back up to the top and work down again. That is Cabernet Sauvignon. He wants the Sangiovese only right now," one of us will shout.

So they nod humbly, and clamber under the wire and between the vines, to a row to the other side, bringing their crates, and find a space to start picking again. The tractor comes, driven by Lorenzo, and a few men on the trailer give us empty crates in exchange for our full ones. That's the procedure. How heavy they are when they are full. I avoid the lifting. I'll leave it to the men.

Actually, if you look closely at the vines, the leaves of the Cabernet are different. Just slightly. The Cabernet Sauvignon leaves are smaller, more serrated. But someone would have to point it out to you if you didn't know. The grapes look identical. Lorenzo doesn't tell us these things. He's focused on just getting it all picked. We have to watch out for the plastic bags instead.

His wine importer Bent, from Denmark once pointed out the difference to me. Now I've learned that too. I'm so fond of Bent - he and his adorable wife and family. Beyond importing our wine to Denmark, they've become our friends and our children's friends. They come every year. If I need to know something about the wine stuff, I ask Bent. I'll get the answer I need. Sometimes husbands aren't always the people to ask especially in stressful times.

But then that's hardly surprising. For a whole year, he will have been working in the vineyard tending to his beloved plants. There's so much manual labour involved in cultivating vines. You have to be dedicated. He says he knows every one of his plants. The harvest *has* to go well. I keep away from him then. I don't bother him just for those days, so I bury myself in the vines and preparing the lunches, so as to avoid any possible friction between us. It's like this year in year out – a pattern so familiar that I almost find his agitated behaviour a comfort.

In some ways, my mother (Shelagh) and he, had more in common with each other than I with my mother. I could never have that passion for the earth like he does. Shelagh did. For that small amount of time they met and knew each other, it was something they recognized in each other. When we got married, Shelagh gave to Lorenzo a music score. It was an anthem sung at our wedding that she had chosen specially for him, for us. She had it leather bound, dark green, and embossed in gold writing:

"To Lorenzo.
Guardian and Gardener
  Of the land he loves
  31 August 1996"

The anthem was by John Rutter, now a favourite composer of Lorenzo's, and was called, 'For the Beauty of the Earth.' We both listen to it occasionally. It is very special to us.

I can't imagine Lorenzo being anywhere else but in the country. To make him sit at desk everyday would be to cut off his arms. I love sitting at a desk. I like writing. I like organizing, creating, thinking, working something out, something on paper - something with words or numbers. Lorenzo - something with his hands. While I will need these to unleash myself from stress or worry (like Sudoku), Lorenzo will calm himself with physical tasks.

He can fix just about anything and takes each problem on board like a challenge. If I tell him the pipe is leaking under the basin in the bathroom of an apartment, or the pump in the swimming pool isn't working and there are flies all over the surface, or some people don't have any hot water in their apartment, he's onto it straight away. He's even opened up the whole swimming pool pump mechanism, worked out the problem, bought the spare part, and fixed it. The same with the boiler. He just magically seems to know what to do. So reliable. As for me, I do these things when I have to – if I'm pushed – but yes, I need pushing. I'll do the easy bit when two people are needed: Lorenzo on the roof with the satellite dish and I'll be half hanging out the window with my neck craned so he can hear me and I can see the television screen at the same time.

"Now?" He'll shout down.

"No, all fuzz."

"What?"

"All fuzz I said!"

"Now?"

"Nope. Still fuzz." Silence. I'll wait some more. "Oh, now yes! No, gone again. Yes, got it!"

I'm there for the children. That's my part. I love helping them understand. I loved being a teacher back in the old days. The relationship thing, the being with people, sharing, imparting knowledge, and the gratification that goes with it.

In this time immersed with my new father Fraser, Lorenzo and I were even closer. Although I was so consumed by

Fraser, I was happy; I had found my father. Lorenzo enjoyed watching me be so happy. I remember one of our rides on his motorbike at the time. Off we went around the windy Tuscany roads. So warm, the wind on my face - bliss - and I clung onto him hugging him tightly, feeling so grateful for him and for everything we had.

My father and I met at Hope's father's airport in October 2008 the same time I was visiting my grandfather. Hope had wanted to come to the airport too; she had made quite a fuss about *her* presence being necessary, necessary for me, at the moment of our meeting. Then she would leave us to it. I never understood this - how it was supposed to help me in such a special and delicate moment. I didn't need her there. Fiona too, had wanted to come and linger somewhere in the background. He didn't want her there either.

So he came alone. I too. I sat waiting for his flight to land and to see him appear from the security doors.

All the fears that I had built up about this moment had gone. Fears about what it would be like, what he would be like, what the reality would feel like after all this ' virtual knowing', and fears too about what he would think of me, whether he'd be disappointed. I found a bench and waited in a meek sort of way. I was thankful it was there because the arrivals hall was oddly empty, and the security doors were set so far back from where I would have to stand, so it felt more comfortable to sit than to be out there so exposed.

It was so different from the waiting, again at an airport, to meet Hope. I had been in love with her or rather, my own invented image of her, for the best part of forty years, right up until, but not after, contact was made. I had fallen in love with my father on the other hand, when contact had *begun*, but not before. My starting point with him had been in real time and with real pictures, a real voice, real words, real thoughts and real feelings. He had never been a figment of my imagination, a ghost image created by me. The only image or expectations I had were the ones he had created himself. Now I was putting the last piece together: to see him in the flesh, putting the voice with the picture, the eyes with the feelings.

So it felt ever so natural to be meeting him at long last. I'd been anticipating this moment for six months. I wouldn't cry, I knew that. I never cry in my own moving moments but I always cry at other people's.

All of a sudden he was standing not more than ten metres away from me. I ran as fast as my legs would go, not unlike in my dream but this time, he didn't drop me. He held me tightly and we hugged. Any onlooker would have noticed the thrill, the excitement, but there was nobody there. Just us. We looked at each other, our faces. He was my father, I was looking into the real eyes of my very own father. I couldn't really believe that I was in the moment, that he was real. It was like I had finally walked on stage for the opening night of a performance after all those rehearsals, but not being able to feel it as the real thing.

We walked across the empty hall, side by side, stealing glances at one another. It was all visual, nothing but. You don't need any other senses for an adoption reunion.

He was smaller than I'd imagined and his eyes were different, not quite so deep set as mine. But he was my father all right. There were no shocks.

We spent the weekend in the city of my beginnings. His city. Hope's city. We drove to the centre from the airport. He pulled over and stopped, and I wondered why. On our right was a grey, quite dirty, tall building.

"This is it, I think. Yes, yes, this is where it all began." He said looking up. I had to crane my neck a bit from inside the car. Forty-three years before he had gone upstairs here with Hope. I felt no sense of astonishment, there was nothing sensational; perhaps there wasn't meant to be. I recorded the moment with a mental shrug. We walked around his McGill University and sat on the grass; that was nice.

As we walked down the streets, the city life buzzing anonymously around us, we chatted like any two people would. The normality felt ridiculous - out of place - and I had to keep reminding myself of the moment.

We passed the church where his parents were married and I suggested we go in. Later, in a busy restaurant, we had a table by a window on the upper floor, looking down over the street and we toasted our reunion. I felt mildly self conscious sitting so close and directly opposite him in full light, but I could tell he felt happy, that he was pleased with what he saw, not disappointed, and he reiterated unabashed that he loved me, loved me just as much now as he had done throughout our long and abstract connection.

After lunch, we went to the cemetery where his family and ancestors were buried. The sun was shining and the leaves had turned – reds and golds against a clear blue sky. It was lovely. There were a maze of paths that wound their way around the neatly cut grass and row upon row of tombstones. It took us forever to find his family spot. There was Maggie, his sister. He brushed away the leaves with his foot to read, 'Who Touched So Many'. Like you, he said, and he held me and told me that he wanted me to feel a sense of belonging – that these people were a part of me. No more floating, he said. He would so like to give me the gift of being able to feel my roots tied to the ground, not just know it, but *feel* it, he said. I couldn't, but willed myself into believing it all. He started looking for more names, telling me all the while who each was.

"Now here's your Titanic great grandparents Stewart and Elizabeth Cawthorn."

My paternal great-grandparents, also from Montreal had a particular love for England, the destination they chose for their honeymoon. They had tickets for their journey home, on the maiden voyage of the new and unsinkable ship, named the Titanic. At the last moment before it set sail, they decided they would like to stay a little longer in England, so cancelled their tickets and came home on another ship two days later.

He had told me the story already but it was funny to see their graves right there in front of me. It was getting quite cold now in the late afternoon, so we left.

He'd arranged a stay in a very glamorous hotel. When I saw my bed, my first thought was that it was so vast it could have slept my entire family. We had dinner in yet another part of town, cobblestones I remember, somewhere by the old port. Talking was easy. I was talking to my friend, my father.

The next morning the fire alarm in the hotel went off. It was so loud, so out of place. I had instant memories of fire practices at school when we were herded out of our dormitory in our nightdresses to huddle in lines outside on the gravel and wait in the cold air for our names to be called. I was wondering if I was supposed to leave the building now. But then it stopped as suddenly as it had started. I was already dressed and ready, having barely slept a wink all night. I phoned him in his room, thinking that he'd have to be awake by now. I was so surprised to be met by a sleepy voice asking what had been the noise he thought he'd heard. Thought he'd heard. I couldn't believe that he'd been asleep. I envied his being able to sleep.

We met for breakfast and as he sat across the table from me, for the first time since being with him, I noticed that there was something discordant about his eyes. It wasn't the eyes themselves – they were very similar to mine – rather, it was the way he used them. While he had been ten thousand miles away in Japan, we had never used Skype, and video calls weren't so much in use then anyway, so we had never seen each other. He had communicated to me so much in his writing or on the telephone, that I felt I knew what was in his eyes anyway. But now, just half a metre away from me, it was as if they did not match the words that came from him – did not hold the same sincerity. It was such a fleeting awareness in the midst of such a perfect time.

We shared a bite to eat at the airport before I left and he talked about Einstein's theories on how the universe has a beginning and an end – how it revolves back round on itself. I found it interesting even in a time like this. He said goodbye to me at security and I felt happy and exhausted. We'd emotionally drained ourselves and I was quite physically worn out too - so much walking. That day we'd been to Westmount, the residential area of Montreal where he and Hope came from, and had walked through the park there, I had seen his old home, his old school, and later, downtown, we had shopped. He'd helped me choose clothes for the children in The Gap, and t-shirts for Lorenzo in

Roots. I'd kept telling myself proudly that I was going shopping with my father; I'd liked that thought - that we were doing something as father and daughter – as if we always had been that.

As we said goodbye, my trust in him was now concrete and I knew that he would be there for me, forever, my father. It was not a new chapter in my life but a whole new book. We would be seeing each other again in just two months. He was coming to Italy with Fiona. He would be in my home with my own family with whom I would share the joy of having found the father that had been missing from my life for so long, and who had now given me so much happiness.

CHAPTER THIRTY-FOUR

Fraser and Fiona's coming to stay with us for Christmas, was above all about celebrating. Celebrating the reunion with my father, and sharing it with my husband and children and with our greater Italian family. Everyone appeared to be excited and moved for me. Also Fiona and Fraser would be jointly welcoming me to their family. Furthermore, being Christmas, it seemed such an opportune moment to meet, I said to Fiona on the telephone. "Christmas I always think is a time for giving and sharing," I went on.

Yes," she replied. It was an empty 'yes' though, said without meaning, - I could tell she wasn't in synch with my thought at all. I felt a fleeting sense of surprise.

I'd told Fraser earlier about Hope's first visit, when she came with her family at Christmas, and that one of the main reasons for it being so disastrous was that the four of them had stayed too long – two and a half weeks. So I was very taken aback when he told me that Fiona had booked the tickets and they were coming for nearly a whole month.

He assured me their visit would be quite different. After all, Fiona just loved organizing and cooking and helping and I wouldn't have to worry. They were not like Richard and Hope he told me, but I knew that already. So I told Lorenzo not to worry about having to entertain my father and Fiona, they'd do their own thing for sure, since they were coming for so long and it would work well. We could meet up every now and again, do some things together but in the main, they would be independent in their own apartment. I imagined they would hire a car but as he'd not mentioned driving up from Rome, I offered to go and pick them up. This meant leaving the house at 5am. My excitement had been infectious and the whole family came. I woke the children early and they came in their pyjamas to get dressed in the car. It was a family adventure as much as anything.

Yet underneath this high, this excitement, I was so afraid of losing him. Both of us were still elated still by our reunion. We were both anxious together about how meeting with everybody else would be.

Yet our situations were not equal: I had found my missing piece – my father, whereas he had not had a space to fill – a missing piece. He had not been looking for his daughter. I was something extra, a new woman in his life, not a daughter he had watched grow up. The important thing for me though was that I had found the paternal love that I had so desperately been in search of.

Once when he was still in Japan, I'd finally asked him why, each time I sent him a picture of me as a little girl, he never made any comment. I'd expected him to tell me what it made him feel – that he was touched - moved - but above all, that he realized how much he had missed. Missed me. However his reply was that he couldn't feel anything at all. The pictures meant nothing to him because he couldn't see *me*, he said. 'Me' was the grown woman he'd come to know. He said he only saw a little girl with no connection to him - this held no meaning at all. A pang of disappointment hit me once again.

But I *was* that little girl. I was the little girl desperately needing my father's love, and yet I was a grown woman with adult feelings. These were new feelings – ones I'd never felt before – which translated into some kind of magical closeness, a closeness that left me in a state of awe. Everything about him and my connection to him was a wonderment.

Complicating matters, there was his wife Fiona. An enigma. Everything he was telling me about her, contradicted my sense of what she truly felt about my arrival into their life. Nothing added up. His praises always constituted excuses for her actress-like behaviour. I was finding it harder and harder to believe that she had not understood what my letter had been saying or that she had forgotten to give it to him. Furthermore, she was not forthcoming about it – it was as if it had never happened, the *how* I'd found him had not existed. In addition she asked little - actually nothing at all - about how I felt when I found him, or when I found Hope. This was plain odd. Not because I thought it should be all about me, but because I was so used to other people's reactions. 'I'm so happy for you', endless questions about how I'd found Hope, or what it felt like when I did, or how long I'd wanted to find my birth parents, and how marvellous it must have been to have found my father now, and so on.

But not Fiona. Not one single question or comment.

At Fraser's insistence, Fiona and I had spoken countless times on the telephone, and conversed by e-mail too. The lack of questions about me - not wanting to know anything about me - was new to me, almost unnatural. It simply wasn't in keeping with my father's descriptions of her – the loving and giving Fiona always thinking of others, *and so excited to meet me,* ready to love me too without conditions, to use his exact words. She talked a lot about herself, she told me *her* feelings, how this reunion had brought out the best in Fraser and had a positive effect on their marriage. She had found her soul mate, she told me, not when she had met and married him, but since he had discovered me.

"You know when you first wrote to me, and you knew, you just *knew* that I was your father, even though I wasn't so sure?" he asked me on the telephone one time when I'd been driving in the car and had had to pull over in order to speak with him.

"Yes," I replied.

"Well, that's how surely *I* know, that you and Fiona will be friends." He insisted. "And I don't mean just quite good friends, I mean that you will develop a really close relationship. I just know it." He was absolutely convinced and stressed every word.

Lorenzo, on the other hand, was not looking for connections. He wasn't looking for anything. He was simply letting all this play out.

We were late arriving at the airport in Rome. It was 8.30am and raining heavily. I held my children's hands as we walked along the arrivals hall. Fiona and Fraser who we spotted from a distance were already out, had their backs to us and were involved with their luggage and trolley.

"By the way, when you come Fiona," I had said to her in the same telephone conversation as the one about the Christmas sharing, "I hope you know we're in the middle of the country here, on a farm and it's quite cold in December. I mean, not freezing or anything, but you'll need sweaters and winter coats. We go for walks and roast chestnuts by the fire and stuff like that. Nothing like being in the city. And we're very informal; you don't need anything smart really. Well, I'm doing a New Year's Eve party, but otherwise, well, it's jeans and keeping comfortable and warm!"

"Oh thanks. Yes I'm glad you said that. I'll know what to bring." She had sounded genuinely grateful.

What caught my eye, before I'd really seen my father with his back to me, was Fiona's coat. It was the colour and texture that stood out – it was shiny and thin, sheet-like thickness, and not at all wintery and warm, and as it moved, its bright copper tones shimmered with the light. It was very long, so that apart from a pair of high-heeled black evening shoes with a little strap and buckle that I could see at the bottom, I couldn't see what else she was wearing. She turned around and saw us before my father did; her face was attractive, tidy and made up.

A minute or so later, having all said hello nicely, enthusiastically, we were still standing in our group, and my father was involved in talking with Lorenzo and the children. I found myself in a separate space alone with Fiona, and instinctively put my arms out to embrace her again, to welcome her, like a message of affection and understanding. It was one of those moments where such a gesture comes automatically

212

without thinking, after all we'd spent time on the telephone, talked about meeting, so an expression of warmth was simply opportune. I put my hand up and touched her cheek. I remember suddenly feeling sympathy for her – I'm not sure why or what gave me that feeling. Did she look alone, like the wife tagging along and trying to be happy when she didn't really feel it? Or did I see fear in her, fear of me?

As I touched her expecting to feel the warmth so long expected, I was most surprised when she just stood stock still, turned her face towards me, and, looking straight at me, narrowed her eyes. Their gaze pierced right through me.

It was simple, unmistakable, contempt.

I couldn't assimilate it though. Not then. Nor in the car as we drove the three hour-long journey back home. In the car, she offered more of the same. I sat next to her in the back and just after driving off from the airport, she turned to face me to answer my question, and I observed an expression of open hostility; nothing in her eye was warm. I began feeling unnerved. She talked at length about her job in marketing for IBM, about how she'd met Fraser and I learned all about their wedding and the rainbow that had appeared when they were doing the photographs. She asked nothing about me, or us.

As for my father, we'd had a quick hello hug on meeting and then, just as he'd settled in the front seat of the car before driving off from the airport, he turned round to face me. He had made an agreement with me that when we would meet all together, he would give me what he described as a 'knowing look', just to reassure me that he was always there for me. I would see everything I needed to see in his eyes alone – no need for verbal communication. In this moment then, it was most odd when, looking at me straight in the eye, he gave me what I can only describe as the kind of nod one might use at an auction to make a bid to the auctioneer, or as a code between sportsmen on the same team. His eye contact reflected precisely this. On receiving this look – this bizarre communication - there was nothing I could manage in return, but a shruggy sort of smile.

Now I could no longer dismiss this strangeness in his eyes. It was here in the car, having not even left the airport, that my excitement about having him to stay and being together, evaporated into thin air. Just like that. For such an unexpected and sharp change in my feelings, I felt altogether peculiar. With the blow of Fiona's communications as well, my head went into quite a tangle, so for the rest of the journey home, I was fairly lost in thought trying to fathom it all out.

Little did I know that what I felt in those first fifteen minutes, was not the innocuous bad start, but just the appetizer for what was to come.

The three and a half weeks rolled along painfully slowly. They didn't hire a car or mention wanting to do so. They didn't ever 'do their own thing' or even eat dinner without us – they were just 'there' all the time. I felt an exhausted sense of frustration when on the third night, my father said to me,

"What time do you want us to appear?" in reference to dinner, yet again. Realizing that this is what he thought was the deal for the next three weeks, I answered,

"Well come whenever you like. Early and then you can help lay the table!" I said. But he looked at me and laughed clearly thinking I was making a joke. They were the guests. We would serve them. The next day I spelt it out to Fiona - Fraser within hearing range - standing by our front door. I told her that I couldn't do dinners like this, not for three weeks anyway, and that it would be nice to share the cooking or take turns. I did have three small children after all. Perhaps sometimes, they could do their own thing, or she was welcome to just open my fridge – all yours, I'd said. She put her hands to my arms giving me a pat and a smile and assured me she had absolutely understood, and that of course she would help and that they were *such* relaxed easy going people, and there was nothing to worry about. I remember feeling quite proud of myself for having been able to express a delicate matter diplomatically, and that I'd got through it unscathed, message received and understood.

But the help never came. They just went on relying on us entirely. Even when we eventually went out to dinner one night, Lorenzo nearly didn't bring his wallet assuming it would be on them. I did too. Even Fiona tried nudging Fraser to pay the whole bill, but my father insisted we go halves. What was he thinking? I felt apologetic towards Lorenzo. Nothing was working. There was nothing I could do. No kindred spirit, no mutual understanding; there was no real laughter either, no letting go and above all, there was no giving.

Meanwhile Fiona avoided being on her own with me. On the second evening I was still in the kitchen finishing preparing this and that for dinner and for a brief moment before Lorenzo and Fraser had come back up from the winery to choose a bottle, Fiona and I were just there together, the children busy with themselves. Instead of staying with me to chat, she meandered in to our sitting room. I could hear her whistling. It was the nervous whistle of someone feigning being relaxed. I went to her and found her uselessly picking up magazines and putting them down again. I wanted to make her comfortable. I found something to say, the men came back, the moment passed.

She kissed my father purposefully on the mouth, and so it went on in this vein, night and day. If we were on a walk, even with other friends, were you to turn round one moment to see who was there, or who was following as one might do, Fiona would be locked in an embrace with my father, looking up into his eyes offering sweet kisses.

One evening, Fraser was already in our house, drink in hand and we were waiting for Fiona to come – she'd been busy with work on the computer. At last she arrived, and I got up to take the glass of wine already poured for her. As I moved forward to greet her, I passed the glass out towards her hand, but she walked straight past me all of a foot away, literally as if I was transparent, and made a bee-line for Fraser, giving him her usual extraordinarily loving kiss as if they'd been apart for weeks, leaving me swaying, glass in mid air. It was all I could do to say, 'excuse me!' The 'laugh line' in a sitcom.

Everything was working backwards. I'd imagined myself having long woman-to-woman kind of chats, where I'd explain and talk about my relationship with my father. I'd imagined warm exchanges of Christmas gifts but she was reticent when she opened the small crystal candlesticks I had for her, and was totally unembarrassed being empty handed for me in return. She had presented no gift to me on arrival either. Perhaps in America they did things differently. While there was nothing for Christmas for me, she had thought of everybody else. For Lorenzo a burgundy coloured sweater she'd picked out, and a black belt, DVD's for the children and lots of little things for Fraser.

What was going on? I had imagined their visit so completely differently. I'd imagined her soft and kind. What was it she had written that summer to me? *'We are so fortunate to have you in our lives and Fraser is the one who has gained the most. I will tell you he has changed a great deal from your relationship with him. He has learned not to take for granted his wife nor his children, and we all have a much more loving and giving man. He is seeing the important little things in life, and I love you for that little bit too*.

But if she had any love at all for me, it was not just difficult, but downright impossible, to detect.

"That was Joel on the telephone," I told her as I came back into the kitchen on Christmas day. "He came here for three months two years ago, because he'd decided he wanted to get to know me, his half-sister. You see he never knew about me either. I can remember how we were two strangers, one to the other. But you know something? Sometimes, you open up your heart more with a total stranger than with others more close to you. Know what I mean?" She agreed. "Well, it was like that with Joel anyway," I went on, "he said he'd never talked like he did with me before. It was just easy to get close with a new person. Just like with Dad and me, and us both opening our hearts to one another." I added, knowing that he'd impressed upon her many a time, the specialness of the relationship he had with me. He'd wanted her to know and understand.

I was sitting in the armchair and she standing near, and on those very last words of mine, I saw Fiona visibly tighten.

My words had unintentionally been daggers, when they were intended to reassure her - to help her be more comfortable with the workings of our reunion, and understand how we had got so close, so quickly, and how it might be normal under such unique and unnatural circumstances, to feel so intense and involved. She needed to understand, if all of this was ever going to work between us. She needed to be able to step back like Lorenzo, and give us time.

But I knew then, that she didn't want to. All she could do was to exert her power - her position - over me.

I didn't know how to treat her any more. I had been gracious to her and kind. I couldn't express anything to her at all. Besides, as far as I could see, her behaviour towards me, and more importantly towards him, was all to no avail, for in as much as she was trying to draw him in, like a fish on a line, he seemed totally oblivious to her, actually quite the opposite, and she would have done better to attract his attention by winning me over instead.

Nothing improved. There was a mild relief when they went to Rome for two days. When they came back, I'd organized a New Year's Eve party with all our family and friends. I'd wanted them to meet my father and knowing how much Lorenzo's family so love to be altogether, for holidays, for any family occasion and it was a good excuse. Fraser made a touching speech about having me in his life and how enriching it had been. Everybody raised their glass and there were smiles all round.

Then Fiona kissed him. She started with her usual kiss on the lips. Then she kissed him again, then again and again. On and on she went, drawing his mouth to her until she started parting her lips to his, tilting her head to one side. She was on the cusp of a full-blown sexual kiss. He stopped her at that point, pushing her off firmly with an apologetic and embarrassed smile.

As the evening rolled on, Fiona drank on too. On most evenings she'd begin to close her eyes as she was looking at you, even early on before we'd even sat down at the table. I thought she was bored. But after they'd left, I discovered a line-up of empty bottles, both spirits and wine, on the floor of their apartment. I had been amazed, for they had been with us most nights and I wondered how it had been possible for her, or them, to drink so much. I later learned from some other friends who came that New Year, that an equivalent number of bottles had been discarded into the bottle bank and then replaced in the supermarket, when they had gone to the village together, for lack of a car.

My mother-in-law had tried talking to Fiona that evening, as others did, but Fiona was making little sense and by the end, she was sitting alone at the table, amongst now half empty glasses and party paraphernalia, her head bowed low over her chest, almost falling onto the table. There were giggles coming from the kitchen. But the saddest part of all was that my father didn't rescue her.

It was the contrast between them that was so apparent, as if my father and Fiona were in two separate boxes and yet right there together - she so terribly drunk with her back to the room and to him, and he, intent only on talking to each and every person at the party, a kind of 'doing the rounds' like a king, as if everybody was wanting and waiting to meet him, the honour all theirs, and, with no need of her, he left her all alone to make a fool of herself as if she was no part of him at all.

One day I suggested a walk, and by chance really, we ended up just my father and I. We walked along the track road I knew well, that lead from the back of our land towards the house of dear friends of ours from New York. They weren't there to drop in on unfortunately. He was telling me his concern about what Fiona was feeling about his relationship with me. I told him he must tell her not to worry, that all was well, and that Lorenzo was perfectly comfortable – simply happy for me.

At the same time, he kept stopping, giving me an embrace that was unnecessarily long, with his face close to mine as if waiting for more. I had the surest feeling that were I to turn my face towards him, he would have tried to kiss me. I didn't like it at all, but felt guilty for not wanting what he wanted and simply pulled myself away and made sure we carried on walking. I was perplexed too that he could want this forbidden thing at the same time he was so worried about his wife's jealousy. I had the sense that he was trying to convince *himself*, as much as me or anybody else, of feelings towards her he simply didn't have.

As we neared home, the first person we saw was Fiona. She'd come out from their front door, pretending not to have seen us approaching. It would have been impossible for two people walking towards the house not be seen. I heard that same nervous whistle I had come to recognize. Could she not bear to see me with him?

She turned around as we called her name, and acted completely surprised and happy to see us.

On Christmas evening, we sat, the seven of us around our table yet again. It was forced, it was false, it was formal. The three 'f's'. Nothing was natural or amusing. Nothing was relaxed.

Then the phone rang. It was Pat, Fraser's younger brother. It was the first time he had ever called, and as I understood it, was longing to hear my voice. He and his wife Margaret, had both been extremely moved by my appearance into Fraser's life. I spoke with them both. They obviously each had the phone to their ear.

While I was standing there, Fiona floated past me and on into the kitchen quietly whispering in my ear on her way, she'd like to have a word with Pat after. As I was closing down the conversation I added, "Oh sorry Pat, just one moment ,Fiona said she'd like a word."

"*Fiona?*" Came a simultaneous reply from each of them. Their tones were of great surprise, as if she should be last person in the world who might want to speak with Pat or vice versa. I was surprised by their surprise. We were all surprised at this point, because Fiona too acted all surprised, when I called to her that Pat was here on the phone for her.

"Oh me? You mean Pat wants to speak to me?" She said in a clear voice as she got up from the table to which she had returned just five minutes before. Apart from Fraser, there was no one but the children and Lorenzo at the table.

As for my father, I don't know what he was seeing. Very little, probably. Perhaps nothing. What were they saying to each other in private? Was the acting going on there too? I couldn't know. All I knew was that she was clever about giving me the glares privately, and making a show of warmth in front of him.

My father and I said goodbye when Fiona was busy with the suitcases and he hugged me tightly. I had the same uncomfortable sensations I'd had when we were on our walk. His face was close to mine, and I felt both guilty and sorry for him at the same time. I would hurt him if I didn't show reciprocal feelings, but I didn't feel what he was feeling. Still, I allowed him to hug me tight. I was repulsed by him and just wanted him to let go, be gone. I recall looking to the side and down to the floor and he brushed away a hair from my face and I knew he understood nothing.

At the station, I dropped them off. We had lunch in a dull bar near the station. At the end, he left the table for the bathroom. I turned to her and gave a friendly caress on her arm, a smile. She was sitting right next to me. I wanted to try at least. But she refused my offer of tenderness – she simply didn't respond and gave me an icy look yet again. I didn't really blame her – her husband was lost to another woman.

Right then, I wanted them both gone. I didn't want to see him either. If he came again, he would have to come alone. I knew I we would not be visiting them in America.

As we waved goodbye, me standing on the platform, she made sure to be kissing him yet again, as if it were she who was saying goodbye to him not me. Her kisses hid me. Lucky, for he would have seen only my sheer relief.

220

CHAPTER THIRTY-FIVE

What happened in the succeeding few weeks, I would never have imagined.

For a month, we awkwardly corresponded. I heard nothing from Fiona. He was no longer in his tiny apartment alone in Tokyo, but in their winter home in Arizona.

I was still reeling. He was not the perfect father that I'd believed in earlier. But I still wanted to have a father. I clung on by way of emails and a call here and there.

Gradually though it became impossible to deny my anger. I felt tricked. Fiona too had tricked me. She was tricking him as well. He wrote long confused emails trying to fathom what was happening to me.

He knew I was angry. I told him that in the future, it would be better if he came alone. I tried explaining that it wasn't so much what she had *done* to me, but rather what she *hadn't* done that hurt.

Initially he was soft and kind. He knew what the problem was he said - she was jealous - but said that it would only be a question of time, and she would get accustomed to all of this. To me. To his feelings for me. All would be calm one day.

I didn't want it be calm one day! I didn't want her to 'get accustomed' as he put it. I didn't want to have to see her ever again.

The point of no return came next. I received an email from him, altogether different from any one I'd had so far, with an attachment of music. Nothing new in that but here was Sarah Brightman singing the melancholy 'La Wally'. He insisted I listen with my eyes closed and think of him. The words were about 'goodbye' forever. He was now 'moving away' he explained. His early love for Fiona had been miraculously restored, his life there in Arizona with her and their friends was something separate and far away from me, but he would never forget his love for me. He said it was like in 'Titanic' where the heroine goes on to live a fulfilling life, but without forgetting the love for the man she had fallen for on board the ship. He insisted I listen to Celine Dion's, 'My Heart will Go On and On', adding that his heart, too, would 'go on and on' for me. Had he turned sixteen?

Then a phone call from him came shortly after.

While I've forgotten the exact words, I can't forget his tone. He had a voice I had never heard before – hard, matter of fact. None of the softness that had been a part of the father I thought I knew so well. It was sort of, 'now listen here young girl' tone, with the words, *'I love you as a father now, but I'm not in love with you any more'*.

But where *was* this love he was talking about? His voice was robotic – as if saying a spiel, prepared.

He explained that he had confronted Fiona about her behaviour in Italy. Fiona had cried. She accused him of not loving her anymore. He had cried too, and now he was reprimanding *me*. This was all *my* fault. They had both suffered so much pain because of me.

As I sat in the armchair in the kitchen, I felt as if I was in another world, neither mine nor his. I was suspended somewhere in mid air. Then, all of a sudden, Camilla came into the room.

"Mummy, when are you coming?"

It was 10pm and my daughter was waiting for me to come and say goodnight. My precious daughter. What could be more important? I had to go to her.

"Listen," I said to my father, "I have to go to Camilla now. It's late. We're not finished. I'll call you back."

I hugged my daughter. I stroked her face.

"Goodnight my girl. I love you."

"I love you too Mummy. Night."

I moved back to the kitchen and as I redialled my father's number, I tried to picture him crying but no image came to me. Later I wondered what trick she had pulled now.

He accused me of completely misinterpreting Fiona, said I couldn't possibly know what she was thinking, and that I had invented it all because of my own jealousy towards her. Fiona had come with nothing other than open arms, she'd tried to make a connection with me, had so wanted to build a relationship, but that I had put up a wall. I had behaved badly, pushed her away, and I had hurt her feelings terribly. The only solution would be for me to reach out to Fiona, admit my mistakes and misunderstandings, otherwise he couldn't have a relationship with me.

It would not be up to him, nor would it be up to Fiona, it would be entirely up to me. At last he had understood everything, he'd thought about it, considered both points of view and Fiona was right. She was such a forgiving and loving person, so wanted the best for each of us. He'd been consumed with me, which of course he now realized was all wrong.

I was dumbfounded. He was ruthless, switching off everything he'd said he'd felt, without remorse, without guilt, so *quickly*. All I managed to ask was why then, had loved me before. He replied, with a tone as if stating the obvious,

"Because I found you attractive!"

It was like he'd pushed me off a wall with his fingertips, to land in a puddle beneath him, and both he and Fiona stood looking down at me in disdain at my sorry messy state.

He never called back.

A couple of months later, he emailed, insisting again on Fiona's version of events. It was just the phone call put in writing. Fiona's truth, now his truth. Fiona so wanted the best for me, he reiterated, and the only way forward was for me to

223

confront my misunderstanding. He ended telling me he still loved me, in a parental way of course.

Once I had hung on his every word. Now I felt only horror. What father would behave this way to his child?

Later that year, his brother introduced Fraser to the term GSA, Genetic Sexual Attraction. Fraser suggested that I too listen to the documentary radio programme on GSA, which might 'help me'.

I listened. It was about adoption reunions turned sexual affairs, a mother and son, brother and sister. I ran to Dott.ssa Pesci in disbelief who in turn was furious.

"He's using this to hide behind!" She said in horror. "What you felt for your father had nothing to do with this!"

How *could* he lie like this? That I was the one who was sexually attracted to him and not he? That I needed help.

For him though, GSA was a credible theory. I couldn't defend myself. Silence was my only way.

Dott.ssa Pesci was furious. She wrote to him:

Dear Fraser,

I am the psychologist Dott.ssa Pesci and as I'm sure you remember, we met in my studio in December 2008. Together with you and your daughter, we had a long discussion about paternal love.

In that moment you seemed very enthusiastic about having found this daughter, and to have met those three wonderful grandchildren and Catriona's husband.

After your departure from Catriona's home, she came to me in a profound state of confusion because she had the impression that your present wife was jealous of her and I understand that she also expressed this to you over the telephone. You later, by e-mail, sent her music in which the words were an "addio". I believed then that you had only sent them in a moment of great sadness because you couldn't accept her criticisms of your wife.

I am wondering now however, how one can give up a daughter, after months of even twice a day, expressing love and joy of having re-found her after so many years, and to have been living her like a blessing.

The love that one gives to a wife is not the same as that which one gives to one's own child. Our children are a part of us and the love one holds for them is eternal; and with a spouse one feels a spiritual and instinctual love which is completely different. The two loves can live one with the other without causing damage to either or anybody. You could live in the joy of a newly found daughter after forty years, give her your name and love her well, just like that.

You have to understand that an adopted child suffers many problems and does not grow on an "emotional plane" like other children. Your daughter has grown very much recently and certainly since having found her birth parents and in particular to have found the father whom she held to and cared about so much. But what happened? With the same speed in which you found her and gave to her, you left her. This does not seem right to me. This woman (and before a child) has been thrown away too many times and I find this unjust and cruel.

If you knew that Catriona would have triggered the jealousy of your wife, you would have done better to not have brought her, because at least you would have brought to life the dream of having a wonderful and kind father with whom she could spend time and share with her family.

Losing Catriona, you lose a wonderful part of yourself, because she is an amazing and very special woman, full of enthusiasm which she transmits to all those who come close to her. I would say that Catriona is a rare pearl, truly precious. She could forever be a place of support in your life, on an "emotional level" which has nothing to do with the radio programme you sent her.

Reconsider and try to be just. Love for this daughter means redeeming forty years of emotional suffering and this could bring about an authentic happiness.

Your wife, if she is truly loved by you, should be able then to live in the shadow of this joy of yours, and it should also be her joy.

I do hope my letter makes you reflect and brings you to recovering the balance and harmony that you had established during your time in Japan.

Distinti saluti, Dott.ssa Anna Pesci

Nothing changed. I knew it wouldn't. He moved from 'GSA' to another term he discovered, 'transference'. The finger always pointed at me. Then he began writing every now and again to tell me to read such and such an article - and to give me a page number from a particular book, to help me understand how I had confused love and approval. He now seemed to have read every book ever written about adoption – it seemed to be his 'thing'. He knew everything about it. Quite the psychologist. All of this was because he loved me as my father, he would always add.

Dott.ssa Pesci was insistent that he give me his name if we were to continue a relationship. We emailed about this and he was keen to meet up with me – we had a lot to discuss he said. I said there was nothing to discuss but that he could give me his name officially – his surname - just as Dott.ssa Pesci had suggested. We could meet indeed for that.

At this, he became even more keen and was enthusiastic about going through the procedure. His name would then appear on my birth certificate. I began to make some enquiries and learned that it was reasonably straightforward. My presence wouldn't actually be necessary but I would come out of respect if he was prepared to do this for me – for us.

I told him I would be coming to England to meet him for this with my family. I would not be coming alone, I wrote, because it was to be a family celebration that he would officially recognize me as his daughter – it wouldn't be about meeting with him alone to discuss our relationship. He didn't answer. His enthusiasm evaporated into thin air. I didn't hear back from him and our communications finished there and then.

From a few family members I'd met or who later contacted me, I heard that he threw his theories around with everyone and anyone who had heard about me – that I was in love with him, jealous, that I wanted him sexually. This was a 'sides' thing for him. Father versus daughter. Everyone had to be on his side. A battle, and he must win. I heard from a cousin of his who came to stay with us, wanting to meet me, that he tried to win over my two half sisters too, who, having despised him for so many years, agreed to meet with a therapist sitting between them. My sisters refused him there and then in the studio of the therapist, telling him they didn't want to see his face ever again, and left the room slamming the door behind them.

CHAPTER THIRTY-SIX

"Which family does this question refer to?" I had asked Dott.ssa Pesci when I was filling in the questionnaire, way back in the beginning before I set out to find my mother.

"The one you have – the one you live with. *Your* family," said as if I'd asked a silly question.

Today I'd know right off what was meant. But then I'd been confused. Yes, there'd been my initial family of four each of us separate from one another, isolated, unhappy. Then in my imagination all along, there was a shadow family with a loving mother, who lived and took shape in my secret heart. But my real family, just as Dott.ssa Pesci had pointed out, was the family that I had created with Lorenzo.

My children are a part of me, a part of Lorenzo and his family. They also are a part of my Shelagh and Nat and Finn family. Although they've lived their whole lives in Italy they are not *only* Italian. I have passed on Shelagh's lessons and values, just as I pass on my childhood, my stories from England. My children hold these stories dear – stories with real events and real people from the past who are connected to me, and so to them, forming their identities.

Family is not blood but history. It is about shared stories. Finn and I shared our two parents. There are things that only he and I could know or feel. "Blood" is a myth. It may offer solace at times of estrangement, but without shared history, it is nothing.

I tried to become a sibling with Hope's sons, Fraser's daughters, but discovered that I could never be that. What *did* we share? Essentially nothing at all, except for some measure of DNA. But DNA I also share with other people – ancestors - I will never meet and certainly can't commit to.

"Tell me that one again about the that tree bridge!" Anna pleaded.

"Well," I began as we sat around the kitchen table. "I had a friend to stay when I was about seven years old. A friend from school. Her name was Nicola. Nicola Reineck."

"Nicola what-neck?" laughed Tom, and all three laughed with each other.

"Well anyway," I went on. " You know we had this river going all around the garden?"

"Yes yes," in unison.

"Well, in the winter, the river could be quite fast flowing and deep. My mum told me it was dangerous. We were allowed to cross over a tree bridge – it was a tree that had fallen from one side making a bridge – by shuffling ourselves along in sitting position. But only when my mum, or dad were there. Well, when I had Nicola to stay, they were going to take the dogs out for a walk and my mum said, 'On no account are you to cross the tree bridge. Ok?' And I promised her that we wouldn't. After playing for a bit, Nicola suggested we go over the tree bridge. I honestly completely forgot my promise to my mother (I was so excited about having a friend to stay) and off we went. As we were both half way across the bridge, who should I see coming towards us on the other side of the river in the field?"

"Your mum!" Camilla said.

"Yes, and I could see the fury in her walk. I knew I would be in trouble. Sure enough, she got to the fence on her side of the river, and said in a really stern voice, 'I'll talk to you when I get home!'. Of course I was terrified. When she came back, she took me into the kitchen telling Nicola to go to my room a moment, and then she pulled down my trousers and pants, picked up the wooden spoon and spanked me so hard! Oh so hard."

"Did you cry."

"Yes. But I sure learned my lesson."

"When can we go there? When can we go and see the house? I want to see it." Tom asked.

"Well next time we're in England – we'll see."

In fact, when we went for Christmas to England in 2011, we stayed in my old town Salisbury, which we had visited many a time with the children before. On one of the days, we drove to my old village, stopped at the church and went in.

"*Questo è dove la mamma ed io siamo sposati. È bello vero?*" Said Lorenzo, putting his arm gently around my shoulder. It's a beautiful church – a mixture of stone and flint, dating back to the 13th century. We all five felt the history as we looked up and around. We felt the past – our own past. Our story.

Back outside we clambered into the car and drove a further half mile along the narrow lane I knew so well. We slowed down as we approached Lower Mill.

"There," I said. "Look, there's the river in front where Finn and I used to catch trout. And there's the bridge my dad built. See?" The children peered forward straining to see. Lorenzo had brought the car to a standstill. We all had our faces turned towards the house. My old home.

There was silence.

I turned to look at Lorenzo and he smiled at me.

I felt an overwhelming sense of calm. And of love.

I had come home.

I learned through Dott.ssa Pesci that: 'if we can dismantle the seemingly inflexible network of our life-long held beliefs, mostly unconscious ones, and then have the strength to reconstruct the beliefs from scratch, we can change the story that dominates our life. We change ourselves.'

If the death of my first family compelled me to find my birth parents, one after the other, it was the stunningly brutal failure of those reunions that impelled me to write it down. To figure this out.

The mother in my mind all those years was never *her* – Hope – but more of a fairy godmother, a good spirit to whom I could tell all, who would always love and guide me, just as Dott.ssa Pesci turned out to be. But because she, the mother in my mind, was non-existent in the real world, she was in essence *me*.

Reunions are risks. There are high hopes and expectations. How can there not be expectations? My worst fear was to find a mother who was a 'down and out', a drug addict, a failure. How could I have imagined that what I did find was worse than this?

I was conceived not out of love or violence or passion but accidentally, without feeling.

Hope gave me away not reluctantly, not in anguish or deep sadness or grief or torments - she was not torn – but with *relief.* Her months long punishment was finished. I had punished her and now she was rid of me. She'd paid her dues.

She never wanted to find me, she never – but once momentarily – gave me a *thought.* And even when she told me this – answering my eager curiosity – it was not a reluctant admission but an indifferent aside – "Oh yes, I do remember thinking one time – maybe she is married now."

Nor did she ever think – "I might have grandchildren somewhere in the world" and – "Oh how I wish I could know them, peek in on them. Oh how I long to know this daughter I couldn't keep." And even when she met these grandchildren – these three little people part of herself – it did not become her mission to create warm memories of a granny.

All of this knowledge – this truth - at first so hard to bear, liberated me. What did I owe her? She couldn't even understand why her blithe admissions crushed me. She never saw *me,* never recognized my dream of a loving mother.

Both of them – alike in this – took pride in me *now.* I'd "turned out well" and now they wanted, or simply felt they deserved, credit. For what? Some genes – genes which were not theirs to own, nor an accomplishment. Genes that come from way back from so many different sources of history. They wanted to take credit for being Canadian too!

They were both oblivious, self-absorbed, and vain. Hope was without guilt, or sorrow and as far as I know, she bore no shame for never wanting to know me. The only shame she felt was towards her hypocritical parents.

Hope and Fraser are not my past and – now I know – are not my future either. We shared moments of knowledge, or recognition, but not connection and no love either. Did we even like each other?

Had I never gone about finding them, I would never have fallen, never been so hurt. Without the fall however, I would never have had to pick myself up - mend. It is this mending which has been my life lesson. We learn more through failure than achievement. And through learning I am stronger, most definitely wiser, and, I hope, a better person.

If there were any battles to be won, they were not with my father, nor with my mother. The battle was simply, always, my own.

EPILOGUE

It is Monday morning 6th September 2011, two or three weeks before the annual 'vendemmia' – grape harvest. It's just before the children go back to school too. We can feel the change - an almost a palpable lull - before the onset of school activities. But also, the quiet exists in the wait for the right moment to pick. The grapes have to be ripe – sweet enough to make the Chianti Classico wine, but still fresh and healthy, no mildew. They're not yet ready. We wait. The hazy summer heat is now off and the days are filled with clear blue September skies.

Today our guests in the apartments seem to be all out for the day, visiting Tuscany sites. Lorenzo is outside somewhere, busy with one job or another – he's never in the house unless it's raining. I am upstairs helping my daughter Anna with some maths homework. I come down from her bedroom in *that* very moment.

'*That*' moment is when the event has already occurred. I hear my telephone ringing. I look. Lorenzo is calling. Nothing unusual. I don't know where he is; maybe he is in the village, maybe somewhere on the farm. I pick up. What does he need now?

"*QUICK! Come down here quick! I'm stuck under the tractor!*"

"Where?" My heart jumps to my mouth as his words register in my head. I hear the fear and the desperation in his voice.

"Down at the bottom of the vineyard below the pool! Quick. Be quick! Run!"

Grabbing my phone, hurling ten words to Tom, our eleven year old son, I run down our steps, rush to the wall to look out to exactly where the tractor could be. I begin the fastest run through the vineyard I have ever done. My heart is pounding. I keep telling myself, 'OK, he's not dead. He was able to call me. He was able to call.' My anxiety is immense. It's bursting from me. I do not know what I will find. My thoughts are of blood, of stemming a flow, of panic. Total panic. What has happened? I have no idea. I know it's bad. My mind races faster than my heart, jumping at possibilities – the worst – prepare yourself for the worst, I always say. Get prepared. My legs pound powerfully down between the two rows of vines, jumping the dry clods of soil, not tripping. I am agile, speedy, intent on my destination. Nothing will stop me now.

I arrive at the tractor from behind. It is facing downhill in front of me. It is still. An enormous piece of machinery with iron rollers and blades is attached to the back looking ready to mangle anything in its wake. The noisy diesel engine is still on.

I see Lorenzo on the ground below the tractor with his foot twisted and caught under the front wheel. His face contorted in agony.

"Get in! Get in and reverse the tractor! Come on! Reverse it off me! Just *do* it!" He shouts, desperate.

The cabin door is still open. I climb up. I sit. I look at all the levers in horror. So many. I am terrified.

"I *can't*!" I cry, but the words are soundless, absorbed by the noise of the tractor. No one can help me. Only *I* can save Lorenzo. I can't face the enormity of this knowledge. I cannot bear the responsibility. The weight is too heavy. I have never driven a tractor. I want to run away. I want to escape. How can I do this? How do I make this beast to go backwards? I can't. I have no idea.

"*I can't do this. I can't do this. I can't do this,*" are the only words that pour repetitively from my lips.

234

"The gear stick on the right! Go on! Just do it! Just do it!" Commands Lorenzo. I press the seemingly massive peddle on the left, to the floor. That's the clutch. Ok, so far. Ok. I find an 'R' on one of the levers on my right. I jerk it down to that position. I put my shaking right foot on the far right peddle. That must be the accelerator. It's huge. There isn't a part of me that is not trembling. My brain is trembling. If I release that clutch, what if I've got it wrong and the tractor jerks forward? My husband is there beneath me. I will mangle him to pieces.

"No, no, no!" my mind races. There is no time. I *have* to let go. I *have* to bring that clutch up. All sound is blocked out. Life stops. I stop breathing.

Perhaps I close my eyes as I begin to release the clutch. I lift the pressure that I am exerting on that peddle. It feels like Lorenzo's life is suspended somewhere between it and the command I give to my leg. I give more pressure on the other peddle on my right, the accelerator.

And in that next split second, the tractor, this strange machine - my adversary - gently, miraculously, obeys.

It backs up. It performs as requested. But of course. It's a machine.

But to me it feels nothing other than a miracle.

It only takes a few centimetres for Lorenzo's foot to be released. I sit still trembling, by now, with my foot so hard pressed down on the brake, as if it's my own leg itself which has the power to hold the tractor firm and still, only my leg, only me. Both sides – clutch and brake. I don't know how to disengage my fierce grip. The engine is still on.

Tom, who couldn't have not noticed the fear, even terror in my voice, my eyes, arrives.

"How do I switch it off! How do I switch it off!" I beg him.

My child, so calm. So sweet. My dear child.

"The key is there Mummy," he replies. So I turn it. The noise abates. There is quiet. Lorenzo rolls over to the safety of the other side of the vines.

The battle is won.

Printed by Amazon Italia Logistica S.r.l.
Torrazza Piemonte (TO), Italy